HOW TO BUILD

BARS

by Donald R. Brann

Library of Congress Card No. 67–15263

SEVENTH PRINTING — 1976
REVISED EDITION

Published by:
DIRECTIONS SIMPLIFIED, INC.
Division of
EASI-BILD PATTERN CO., INC.
Briarcliff Manor, N.Y. 10510

FIRST PRINTING
© 1969

REVISED EDITIONS
1970,1971,1972,1973,
1974,1975,1976

ISBN 0-87733-690-3

NOTE
Due to the variance in quality and availability of many materials and products, always follow directions a manufacturer and/or retailer offers. Unless products are used exactly as the manufacturer specifies, its warranty can be voided. While the author mentions certain products by trade name, no endorsement or end use guarantee is implied. In every case the author suggests end uses as specified by the manufacturer prior to publication.

Since manufacturers frequently change ingredients or formula and/or introduce new and improved products, or fail to distribute in certain areas, trade names are mentioned to help the reader zero in on products of comparable quality and end use.   The Publisher.

Shift Your Mental Gears

Those who research human behavior continually reveal many interesting and helpful facts concerning the way we live, or begin to stop living. A case in point is the level at which people, even those blessed with above average intelligence and income, begin to slow down, withdraw, instead of expanding their physical and mental activities with each passing year.

Like flowers that blossom and wither after so many days of growth, people, even in their mid-thirties, stop growing early in life. An enormous percentage, by their own admission, have no desire to shift gears.

Learning to live is life's most important art. No matter how you rate your past, the future is still yours to shape. Building a bar may seem like a trivial way to shift gears, but it does offer a change of pace, an opportunity to broaden your sphere of activity. Invest time in any constructive endeavor and you'll find it pays big dividends. See how quickly it helps you reach other goals.

Don R. Bann

CONTENTS

HOW TO BUILD A TV BAR

Building a bar provides hours of complete relaxation plus a fun way to save money. Since all materials only cost a fraction of the price paid for a bar purchased ready-made, a profitable part time business can be developed with the smallest possible investment.

Step by step directions explain how to build a straight or L-shaped bar, a folding cabinet door bar, a TV bar on casters, a table designed for bar use, plus wine storage racks and walls.

The straight bar, Illus. 1, 2, can be built three different ways. As shown, or with a footrest base, Illus. 21, or on casters.

Always read directions through completely before starting to build a project. For greater strength and rigidity, apply white glue to plywood and wood parts before fastening.

Measuring 5'0" long, and standing approximately 43" high on easy-to-roll casters, this bar provides a perfect home for a table top TV set, plus ample storage space for glasses, bottles and other essentials. While directions specify 15" wide shelves, these can be altered to accommodate a wider set, or the TV can project over back of shelf. Alter height of middle shelf if required.

After you begin assembly, measure size of inner parts before cutting. In this way, you can compensate for any variation in construction.

The height of middle shelf and size of sliding panel doors is optional. We placed the shelf and specified size doors that could accommodate a 19" and some 21" portables. Measure overall height of your set and position shelf accordingly. Make a full size paper pattern of the screen, plus controls, if same are on the front. Use this to make cutout in front.

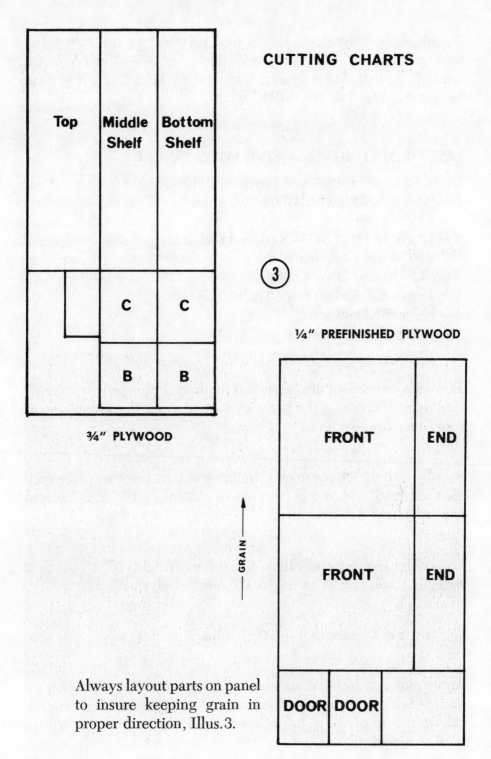

CUTTING CHARTS

③

Top | Middle Shelf | Bottom Shelf

C | C

B | B

¾" PLYWOOD

¼" PREFINISHED PLYWOOD

← GRAIN →

FRONT | END

FRONT | END

DOOR | DOOR

Always layout parts on panel to insure keeping grain in proper direction, Illus. 3.

To establish dimensions, we figured plywood as measuring full thickness, i.e., ¼" plywood — ¼" thick; ½" — ½" etc. When it comes to lumber, 1x3 is figured as measuring ¾" x 2½". If you cut ¾" plywood for 1x3, cut to 2½" width.

LIST OF MATERIALS — FIVE FOOT TV BAR

1 — ¼" x 4' x 8' Prefinished Hardwood Plywood
1 — ¾" x 4' x 8' Plywood Good Two Sides
4 — 2¾" Casters
4 — 1" x 3" x 12' — S4S — Surfaced four sides
18" x 60" Plastic Laminate
1 pr. ¾" Round Door Knobs
5 ft. length ¼" Sliding Door Track
4 — ½" x 36" Dowels
16' picture frame molding

The wide assortment of prefinished hardwood plywoods now available permits finishing the bar with a wood grain that complements your other furnishings.

Step-by-step directions suggest building end frames that place middle shelf 18½" below top. This places center of a 19" to 21" screen approximately 33" from floor.

Use 1x3 for framing ends, Illus. 4. Cut four uprights 38¾", six cross rails 10 ", and one ¾" x 10 " x 12" piece of plywood.

Cut two A — 15"; two AA — 54½", Illus. 5, from 1x3.

Apply glue and fasten cross rails and plywood panel in position indicated with ⅜" corrugated fasteners. Use three fasteners on each side to secure plywood in position. Check and hold frame square until glue sets.

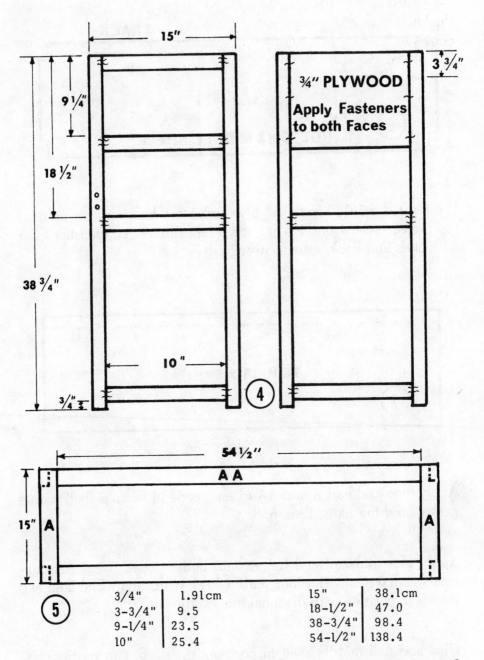

3/4"	1.91cm	15"	38.1cm
3-3/4"	9.5	18-1/2"	47.0
9-1/4"	23.5	38-3/4"	98.4
10"	25.4	54-1/2"	138.4

Cut bottom and middle shelf 15″ x 59½″, Illus. 6, from ¾″ plywood. Notch ends to receive frames. Since we suggest cutting bottom, middle and top shelves from 48″ panel, the shelves will be slightly less than 15″ and 18″ due to saw cuts.

11

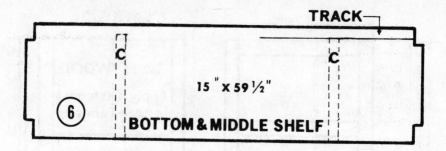

Cut top 18" x 59½" from ¾" plywood. Dash lines indicate amount top projects over front. Do not notch top, Illus. 7. Top finishes flush with ends and back, extends over front.

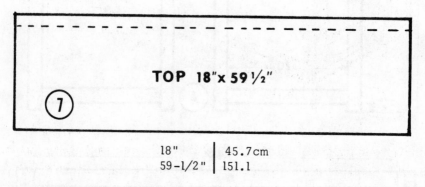

18"	45.7cm
59-1/2"	151.1

Apply glue and nail A and AA to underside of bottom shelf with 4 penny finishing nails, Illus. 5, 8.

Apply glue and nail end frames into bottom shelf; cleat A to uprights with 6 penny finishing nails. Check with square and hold end frames in position with diagonal braces, Illus. 9.

Glue and nail middle shelf in position, then top. Cut partitions C 14¼" wide by 18½" high, or height set requires, from ¾" plywood. Glue and nail in position indicated 15" from end. Keep partition C flush with back of shelf. This provides ¾" clearance for sliding door track across front.

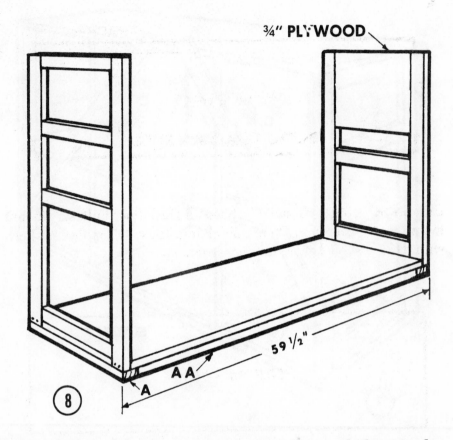

¾" PLYWOOD

59 ½"

A A

A

8

While lower partitions B are also shown 15" from end, these can be placed 1" further away from center to permit nailing down through middle shelf. Cut B to height required by 15" width. Apply glue and nail in position with 6 penny finishing nails. If you want to line up partitions, drive nails in on an angle through middle shelf.

Cut one front shelf support D, Illus. 10. Use 1x3 cut to length required. Glue and nail in position. Nail up through bottom shelf, down through middle shelf.

Install ¼" single sliding door track in position, Illus. 10 and 11, flush with front edge of middle shelf. Track extends to end frames. Use screws or nails provided by track manufacturer. Place wide edge track at top, narrow edge at bottom.

13

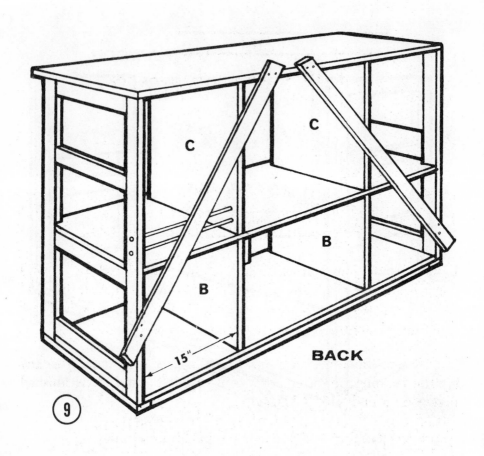

C

C

C

B

B

15"

BACK

(9)

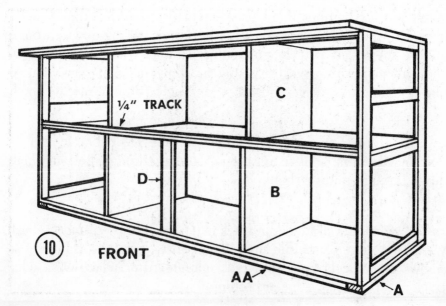

¼" TRACK

C

D→

B

(10) **FRONT**

AA→

→A

14

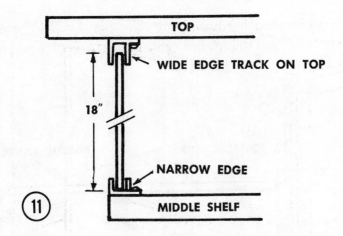

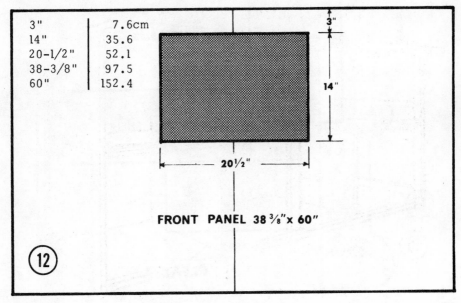

TOP

WIDE EDGE TRACK ON TOP

18"

NARROW EDGE

⑪ **MIDDLE SHELF**

Drill ½″ holes through end frame, 1″ in from edge, Illus. 4. Drill one 1½″ above shelf, the second 3″ up from shelf. Also drill ½″ holes ⅜″ deep in partitions. Apply glue and insert ½″ dowels. These act as bottle guards, Illus. 9.

The picture frame molding shown in Illus. 13, is optional. Use any picture framing preferred. If you use EB#28, cut ¼″ prefinished plywood for ends, 15″ x 37⅝″.

Apply panel adhesive and secure end panels in position.

3″	7.6cm
14″	35.6
20-1/2″	52.1
38-3/8″	97.5
60″	152.4

3″

14"

20½"

FRONT PANEL 38 ⅜″x 60″

⑫

Cut two ¼″ prefinished hardwood plywood panels, 38⅜″ x 30″, Illus. 12, or size required to face bar. Butt panels at center and temporarily tack in place.

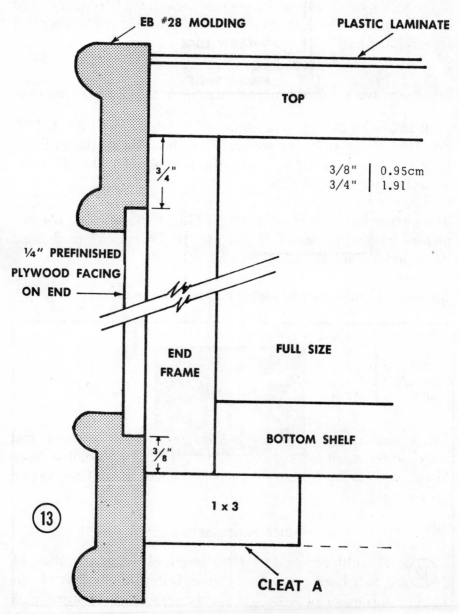

EB #28 MOLDING

PLASTIC LAMINATE

TOP

¾″

| 3/8" | 0.95cm |
| 3/4" | 1.91 |

¼″ PREFINISHED
PLYWOOD FACING
ON END

END
FRAME

FULL SIZE

BOTTOM SHELF

⅜″

1 x 3

⑬

CLEAT A

Using paper pattern cut to overall size of TV screen, cut opening in front panel in position your set requires. The table top portable we installed required cutting a 14″ x 20½″ opening 3″ down from top.

Since position of tuning controls varies, some being on front, side, or top, cut opening sufficient size to permit tuning. Remember, most fine tuning controls located on side or back of set can be operated from back of bar.

Sets that have a pull out antenna require two holes in countertop.

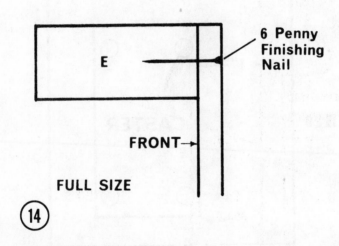

Cut prefinished plywood for sliding doors. Select plywood that matches grain and color of cutout. We cut two 14x18 sliding doors. Slip doors into top track, then drop into lower track. Trim doors if necessary.

Cut 1x3 to width required for E, to length of countertop, Illus. 14. Glue and nail front panel to E. When fastening any part of prefinished surface of plywood, sandpaper area before applying glue.

Apply glue to top of E and to framing that butts against front panel. Nail E to countertop overhang, brad face panels in position to shelves, ends and D. Countersink heads of brads and fill holes with matching Putty Stik.

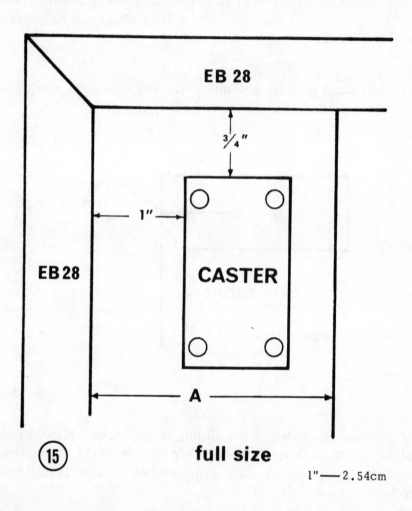

EB 28

3/4 "

1"

EB 28

CASTER

A

⑮ full size

1"——2.54cm

Miter-cut end of EB#28 Molding, Illus. 15. Measure and miter cut to length required to face top edge and ends, also across front and ends at bottom. Notch in molding receives 1/4" prefinished plywood. Apply glue and nail molding in position with 4 penny finishing nails, Illus. 13 and 16.

Cut strips of prefinished plywood to width and length required to face bottom side of countertop, Illus. 16. Apply glue and brad in position end-to-end.

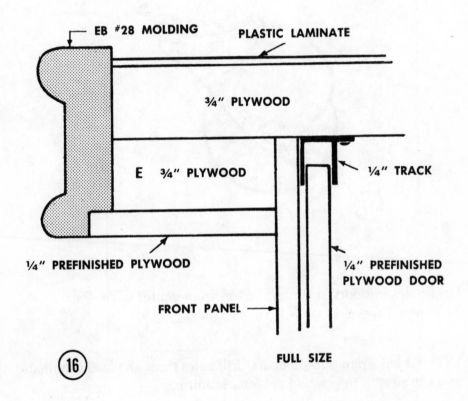

Cut a piece of matching wood grain, white, or color plastic laminate desired, to size countertop requires. Apply with contact cement or with cement plastic laminate manufacturer recommends.

Fasten four 2¾″ casters, Illus. 17, to A with ¾″ No. 6 roundhead screws in position indicated, Illus. 15.

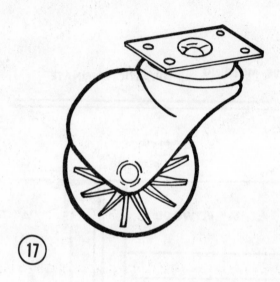

Drill holes in doors at center, ½″ in from center edge. Fasten two ¾″ round brass door pulls to doors, Illus 2.

If TV set has a pair of rabbit ears, drill holes through plastic laminate and countertop in position antenna requires.

BAR EQUIPMENT DRAWER

Illus. 18, 19 shows construction of a drawer. Use ½″ plywood for sides, front and back. Overall width of assembled drawer should be ¼″ less than space between C and end frame. This allows ⅛″ clearance on both sides.

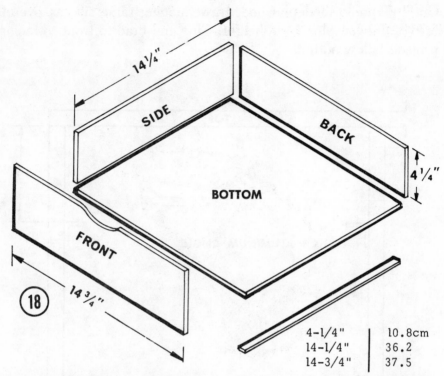

SIDE

BACK

14¼"

4¼"

BOTTOM

FRONT

14¾"

(18)

4-1/4"	10.8cm
14-1/4"	36.2
14-3/4"	37.5

Glue and nail sides to front and back. Glue and nail ⅛" hardboard or ¼" plywood to bottom. Cut ⅛" x 1" x length required, hardwood or hardboard strips for runners, Illus. 19. Glue and brad to bottom.

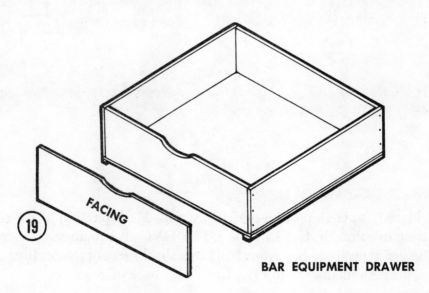

FACING

(19)

BAR EQUIPMENT DRAWER

Cut ¼″ prefinished plywood drawer facing same size as overall face of drawer, plus 1″ in height. Glue and brad to front so facing projects below bottom.

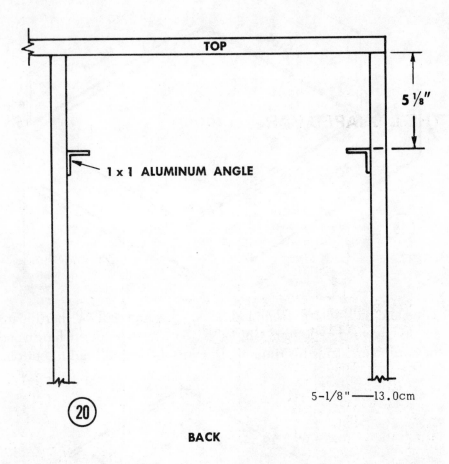

TOP

5 ⅛″

1 x 1 ALUMINUM ANGLE

20

5-1/8 "——13.0cm

BACK

Place drawer in position ½″ below top. Mark position of runners. Remove drawer. Cut ⅛″ x 1″ x 1″ x 14¼″ aluminum angle. Screw angle in position. Recess end ¼″ from back edge of frame, Illus. 20. This permits drawer to close flush with back edge of top.

THE L SHAPED BAR

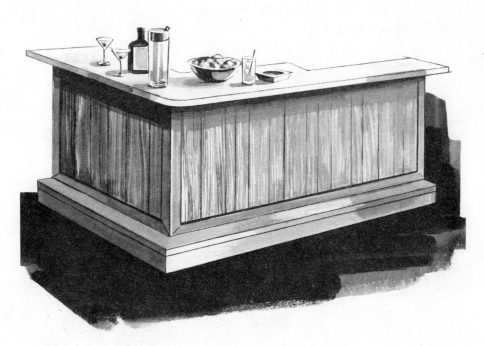

LIST OF MATERIALS

2 — ¾" x 4' x 8' Fir Plywood
2 — 1" x 4" x 8'*
2 — 1" x 3" x 8'*
1 — pair semi-concealed cabinet door hinges for ¾" flush door
1 — door catch
Plastic laminate to cover countertop, shelf M and foot rest
26 lineal ft. — ½ x 1 Stainless Steel Edge Molding
¼ lb. — 3 penny finishing nails.
1 box 1" wire nails
24 — 1¼" No. 8 flathead wood screws
1 — Cabinet Door Lock for ¾" Flush Door
1 — ¼" x 4' x 8' prefinished hardwood plywood**
1 — ¼" x 4' x 4' prefinished hardwood plywood**
1 — sink**

*1x4 and 1x3 can be cut from ¾" plywood
**OPTIONAL

BACK

Step-by-step directions explain how to build an L-shaped bar, Illus. 22, measuring 72" x 39⅛", Illus. 23.

24

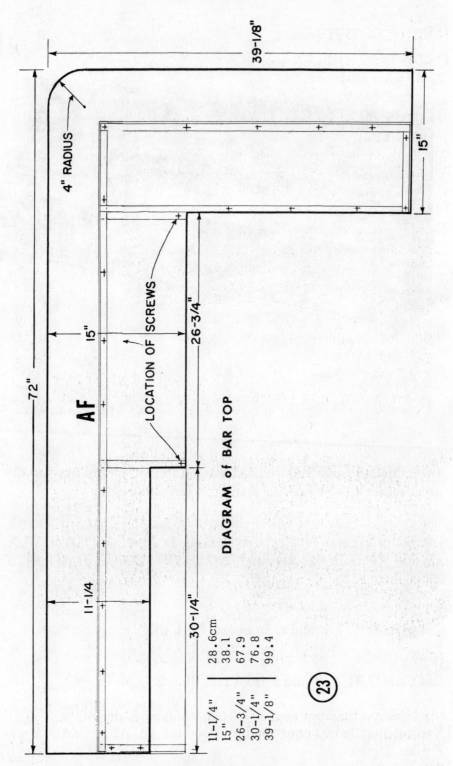

DIAGRAM of BAR TOP

39-1/8"

4" RADIUS

15"

72"

15"

AF

LOCATION OF SCREWS

26-3/4"

11-1/4

30-1/4"

11-1/4"	28.6cm
15"	38.1
26-3/4"	67.9
30-1/4"	76.8
39-1/8"	99.4

㉓

25

(24)

Since this bar is built in two sections, either can be built to size desired; either can be built as a straight bar, Illus. 24.

Directions suggest cutting parts A, B, C, D, M, N, P, Q, R, S, W, X, AE and AF from ¾″ plywood. NOTE CUTTING CHART, Illus. 25, 26.

Cut parts E, F, J, K and U from 1x4, Illus. 27.

Cut parts G, H, L, T and V from 1x3, Illus. 28.

Use ¼″ prefinished hardwood plywood for AA, AB, AC, AD, Y and Z, Illus. 29, 30.

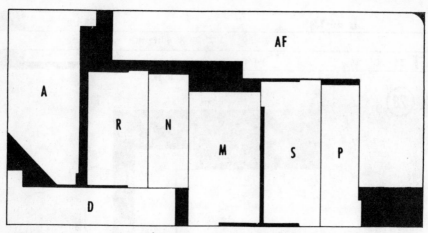

25   3/4" X 4 X 8 ft. plywood

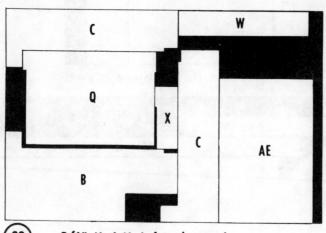

26   3/4" X 4 X 6 ft. plywood

E 69-7/8"	**K** 20-3/8"

1 X 4" X 8 ft.

F 37-3/4"	**U** 36-1/2"	**J** 13-1/8"

1 X 4" X 8 ft.

27

3/4"	1.91cm	37-3/4"	95.9cm
4"	10.2	69-7/8"	177.5
13-1/8"	33.3	4'	121.9
20-3/8"	51.8	6'	182.9
36-1/2"	92.7	8'	243.8

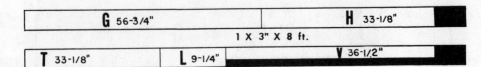

G 56-3/4" H 33-1/8"

1 X 3" X 8 ft.

T 33-1/8" L 9-1/4" V 36-1/2"

1 X 3" X 8 ft.

(28)

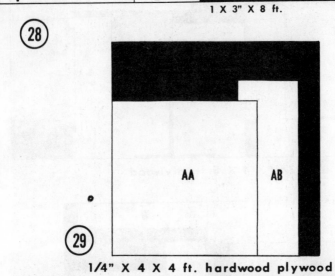

AA AB

(29)

1/4" X 4 X 4 ft. hardwood plywood

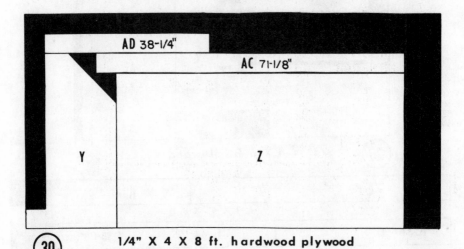

AD 38-1/4"

AC 71-1/8"

Y Z

(30)

1/4" X 4 X 8 ft. hardwood plywood

1/4"	0.64cm	38-1/4"	97.2cm
3"	7.6	56-3/4"	144.1
9-1/4"	23.5	71-1/8"	180.7
33-1/8"	84.1	4'	121.9
36-1/2"	92.7	8'	243.8

28

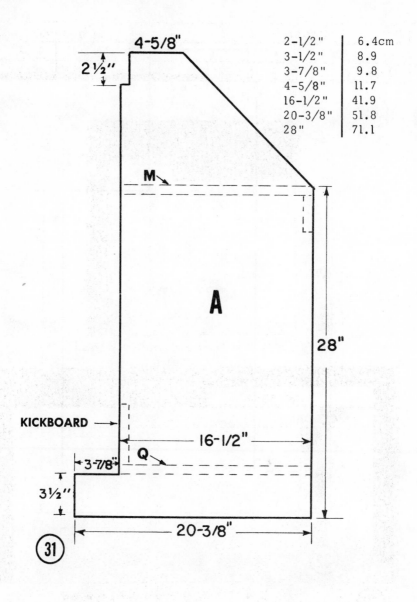

2-1/2 "	6.4cm
3-1/2 "	8.9
3-7/8 "	9.8
4-5/8 "	11.7
16-1/2 "	41.9
20-3/8 "	51.8
28 "	71.1

To simplify specifying dimensions, plywood is figured as measuring thickness indicated. 1x4 is figured as measuring ¾″ x 3½″; 1x3 as ¾″ x 2½″.

Cut one A to size and shape shown, Illus. 31. Notch top 2½″ to receive 1x3 G.

29

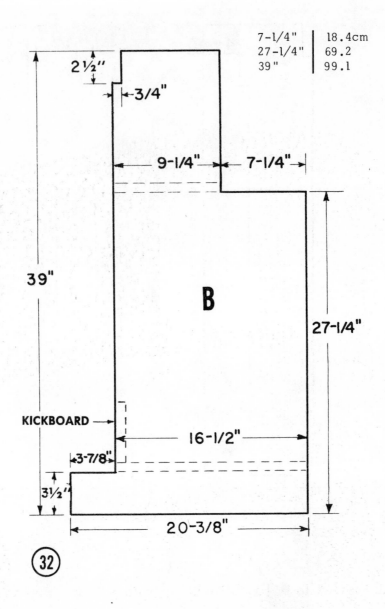

7-1/4"	18.4cm
27-1/4"	69.2
39"	99.1

Cut one B, Illus. 32; two C, Illus. 33; one D, Illus. 34. Cut one E — 1x4x69⅞". One F — 1x4x37¾". One G — 1x3x56¾". One H — 1x3x33⅛". One J — 1x4x13⅛". One K — 1x4x20⅜". One L — 1x3x9¼". Notch A, B, C to size G requires. Notch C1 and D to receive H.

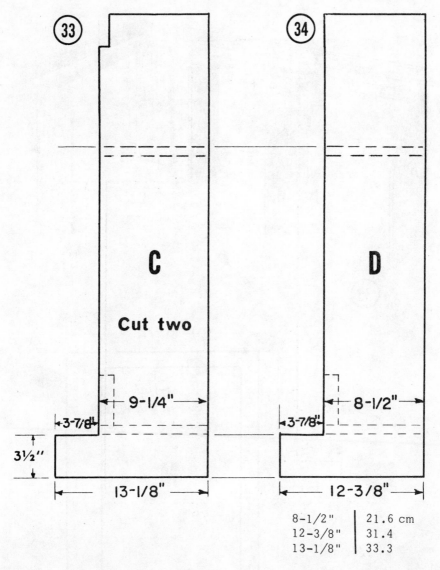

8-1/2"	21.6 cm
12-3/8"	31.4
13-1/8"	33.3

Nail K and L to B; J to C1, Illus. 35, with 3 penny nails. Nail G to ABC; H to C1 and D.

Cut one M, Illus. 36; one N, Illus. 37; one P, Illus. 38; one Q, Illus. 39; one R, Illus. 40; one S, Illus. 41, to size required or size specified. If you don't have a saber saw, drill ¾" holes in corner of M, Illus. 36. Cut opening to size sink manufacturer specifies using a keyhole saw.

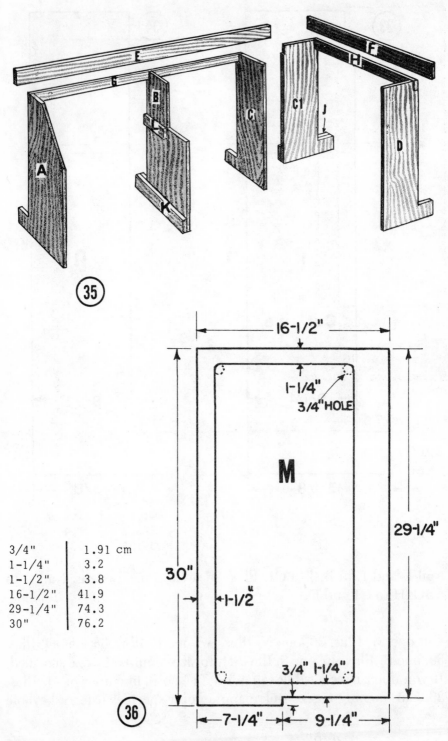

3/4"	1.91 cm
1-1/4"	3.2
1-1/2"	3.8
16-1/2"	41.9
29-1/4"	74.3
30"	76.2

16-1/2"

1-1/4"

3/4"HOLE

M

29-1/4"

30"

1-1/2"

3/4" 1-1/4"

7-1/4"

9-1/4"

35

36

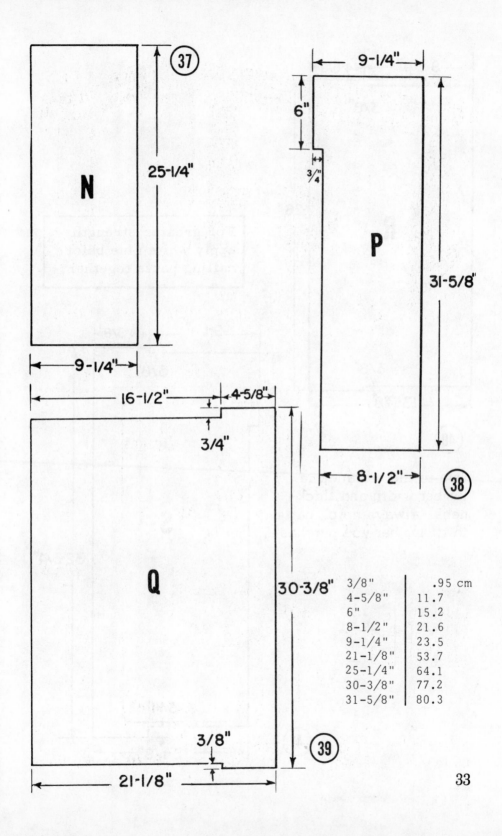

37

N

25-1/4"

9-1/4"

9-1/4"

6"

3/4"

P

31-5/8"

8-1/2"

38

16-1/2"

4-5/8"

3/4"

Q

30-3/8"

3/8"

21-1/8"

39

3/8"	.95 cm
4-5/8"	11.7
6"	15.2
8-1/2"	21.6
9-1/4"	23.5
21-1/8"	53.7
25-1/4"	64.1
30-3/8"	77.2
31-5/8"	80.3

33

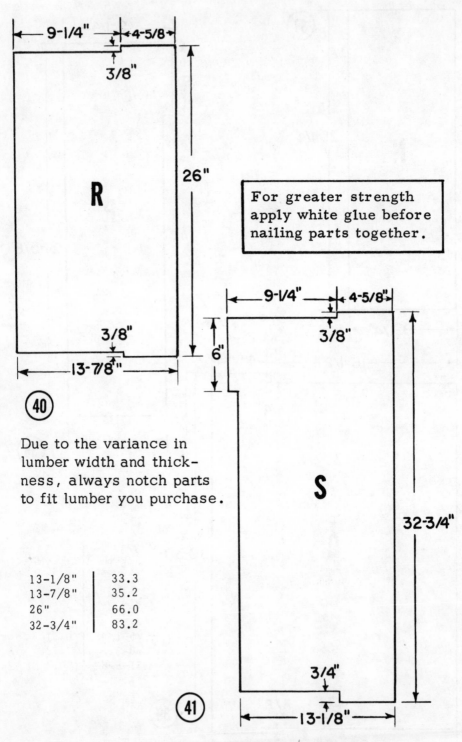

9-1/4" 4-5/8"

3/8"

R

26"

3/8"

13-7/8"

40

For greater strength
apply white glue before
nailing parts together.

9-1/4" 4-5/8"

3/8"

6"

S

32-3/4"

3/4"

13-1/8"

41

Due to the variance in
lumber width and thick-
ness, always notch parts
to fit lumber you purchase.

13-1/8"	33.3
13-7/8"	35.2
26"	66.0
32-3/4"	83.2

Nail E to A, K, C; F to C1, J, D in position shown, Illus. 42. Nail C and B to R and N; R to E; A to M; M to B and L; A to Q; Q to K and E. Nail C1 and D to P and S in position shown. Cut one T — 1x3; one U — 1x4; one V — 1x2.

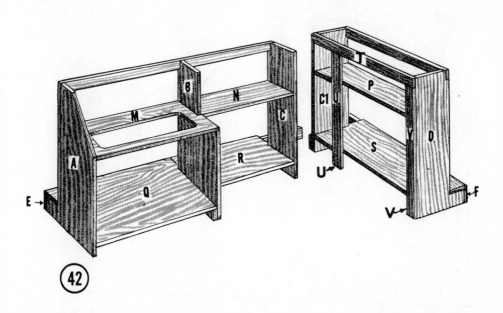

(42)

Nail T to C1 and D; U to P, S; toenail to T; V to D, S and P, Illus. 42.

Cut W to size indicated, Illus. 43, or size required. Nail in position.

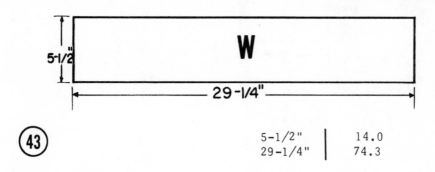

(43)

| 5-1/2" | 14.0 |
| 29-1/4" | 74.3 |

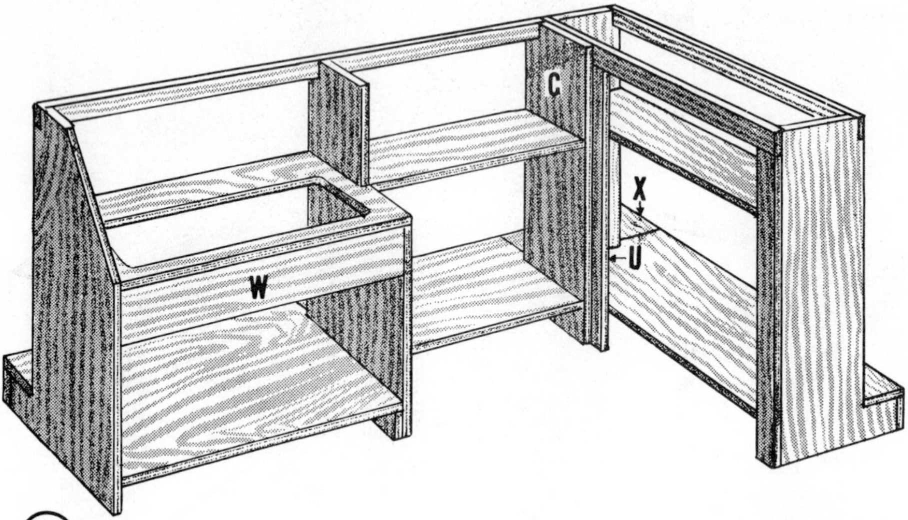

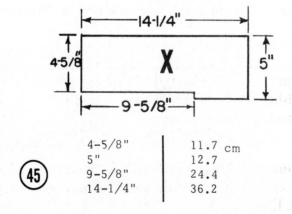

(44)

Nail two units together through U and T into C; through F into E, Illus. 44. Cut X to size indicated, Illus. 45, or size required. Nail in position, Illus. 44.

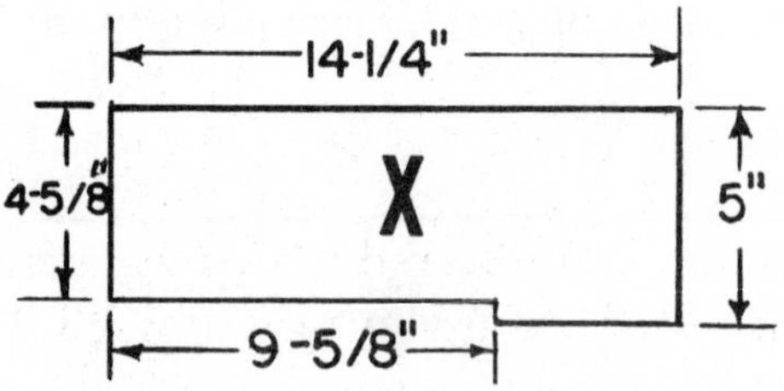

4-5/8"	11.7 cm
5"	12.7
9-5/8"	24.4
14-1/4"	36.2

(45)

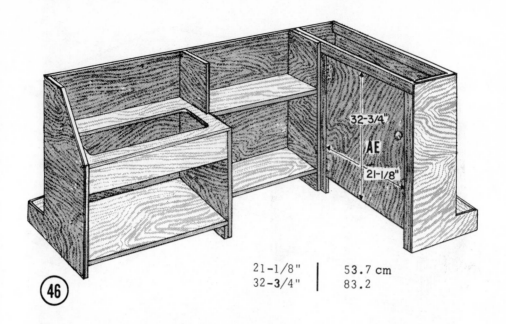

21-1/8"	53.7 cm
32-3/4"	83.2

Cut door AE to size your construction requires, Illus. 46. Hinge in position with semi-concealed cabinet hinges for ¾" flush door. Install magnetic cabinet door catch and/or lock.

Cut top AF, Illus. 23, 47, to size and shape shown. Drill ⁷⁄₆₄" holes where screw holes are indicated, Illus. 23. Apply glue and fasten AF in position with 1¼" No. 8 flathead wood screws, Illus. 47A.

Cut plastic laminate to size required and apply with adhesive laminate manufacturer recommends. Cover edges with ½" x 1" metal edge molding.

The bar can be painted, wallpapered with travel posters, or paneled with ¼" prefinished hardwood plywood, Illus. 48, Miter one edge, then measure exact length required.

If you plan on entertaining heavy footed bar patrons, cut a ¾" x 5½" kickboard to length required, and nail between A and B, B and C, C and D, Illus. 31, 32, 33.

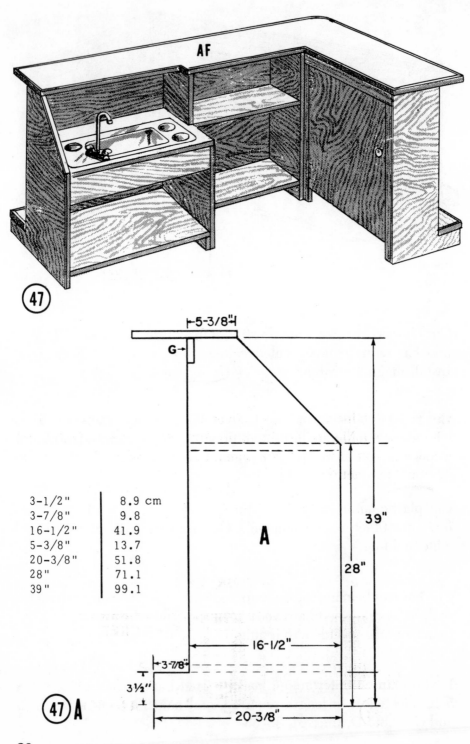

AF

47

3-1/2"	8.9 cm
3-7/8"	9.8
16-1/2"	41.9
5-3/8"	13.7
20-3/8"	51.8
28"	71.1
39"	99.1

5-3/8"

G

A

39"

28"

16-1/2"

3-7/8"

3½"

47 A

20-3/8"

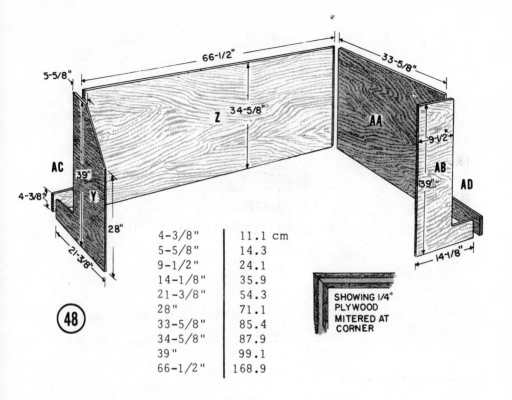

4-3/8"	11.1 cm
5-5/8"	14.3
9-1/2"	24.1
14-1/8"	35.9
21-3/8"	54.3
28"	71.1
33-5/8"	85.4
34-5/8"	87.9
39"	99.1
66-1/2"	168.9

SHOWING 1/4"
PLYWOOD
MITERED AT
CORNER

If you plan on installing a sink, cover M with plastic laminate. Then cut opening in M to size sink manufacturer recommends. Install sink using brackets and clips sink manufacturer supplies, Illus. 49, following manufacturer's directions.

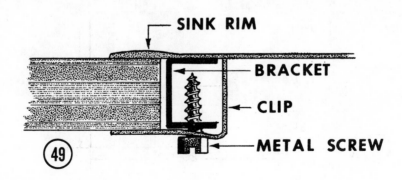

SINK RIM

BRACKET

CLIP

METAL SCREW

OPTIONAL
(50) **HOSE CONNECTION**

Water lines can be connected the same way a washing machine is installed, Illus. 50, or with ⅜″ speedy riser, Illus. 51.

Book #682, How to Install an Extra Bathroom, explains how to install water and waste lines in a professional manner.

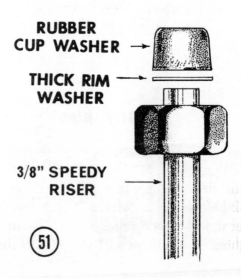

RUBBER CUP WASHER →

THICK RIM WASHER →

3/8″ SPEEDY RISER →

(51)

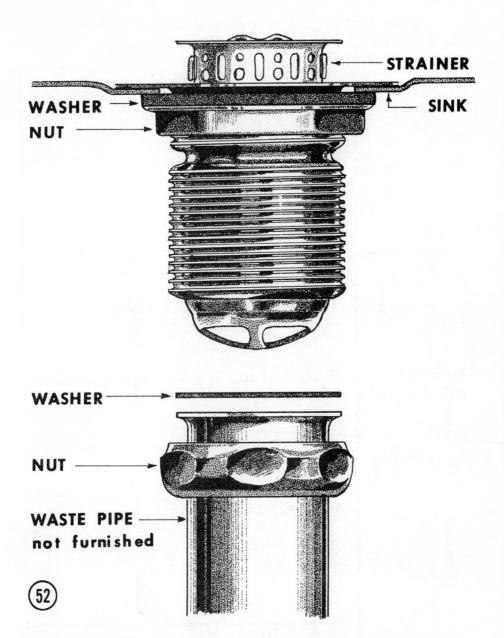

STRAINER

SINK

WASHER

NUT

WASHER

NUT

WASTE PIPE
not furnished

(52)

Install sink drain, Illus. 52. Apply a ribbon of non-hardening putty to recess in sink before placing drain in position. Washer and nut are placed under sink in position shown. Use nose or handles of pliers to turn and tighten drain. Fasten waste pipe to sink with nut and washer shown.

41

Apply plastic laminate to foot rest. Finish edge with stainless steel molding available from your laminate retailers, Illus. 53.

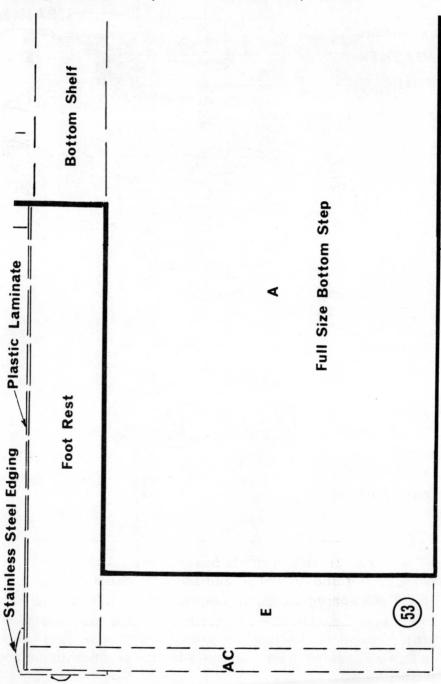

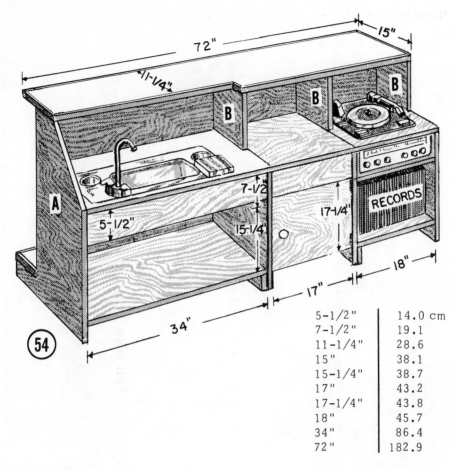

5-1/2"	14.0 cm
7-1/2"	19.1
11-1/4"	28.6
15"	38.1
15-1/4"	38.7
17"	43.2
17-1/4"	43.8
18"	45.7
34"	86.4
72"	182.9

Following the same general procedure, a straight bar can be built to size desired. Illus. 54 shows a bar equipped for stereo. Speaker enclosures are placed independent of bar.

Illus. 21 shows the **L Shaped Bar** finished with prefinished plywood and framed with #41 panelmold or equal hardwood molding.

CABINET BAR ON CASTERS

This handsome cabinet on casters will enhance the decorative scheme of any room. When opened, it dispenses the kind of interior decoration a good host enjoys serving. Ample space is provided for bottled goods, glasses, ice bucket and bar equipment. Its unique design provides a place for everything that's needed, even a refuse drop and bucket.

LIST OF MATERIALS

2 — ½" x 4' x 8' plywood D, E, F, G, H, M, N, P, S, T
1 — 1" x 4" x 12' — A, B, C, O
1 — ½" x 1" x 6' oak or other hardwood — U, V
1 — ¼" x 4' x 8' prefinished hardwood plywood K, L, glass racks, sliding doors.
¼ lb. 3 penny finishing nails.
1 lb. 6 penny finishing nails.
1 box 1¼" wire brads
1 box 1" wire brads
1 box ¾" wire brads
42 — 1¼" No. 10 flathead wood screws
18 — 1½" No. 6 roundhead wood screws
Plastic Laminate — 30" x 36"
6 ft. Stainless Steel Edging
6 ft. ¼" stainless steel quarter round
Two 3' one 4' length of 1½" continuous hinge
4 2¾" casters
1 — hook and eye
1 — door lock — OPTIONAL

We recommend building this bar with ½" fir plywood good two sides. This can be stained, antiqued, or appliqued with molding to create the Spanish decor, Illus. 57. Or you can panel D, E, M, N, T with ¼" prefinished hardwood plywood. All exposed edges can be finished with matching wood tape.

CUTTING DIAGRAMS

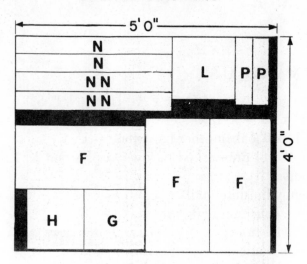

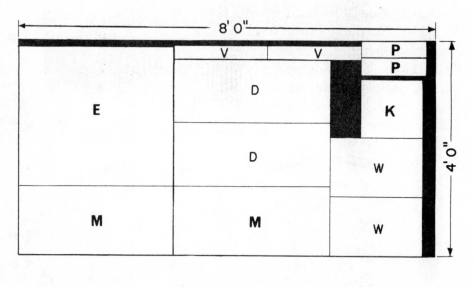

56

4'	121.9 cm
5'	152.4
8'	243.8

Build base to overall size indicated, Illus. 58. Use 1x4 for A, B, C. Glue and nail A to B with 6d finishing nails. Glue and nail A and B to C flush with bottom edge of A and B with 6d finishing nails. Check and brace base square.

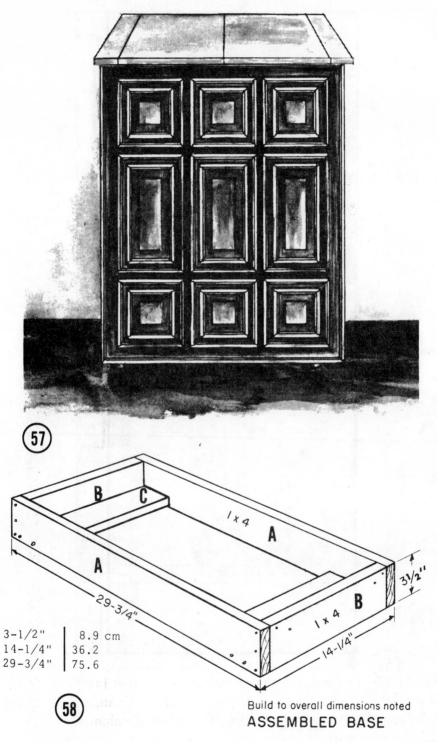

(57)

(58)

3-1/2"	8.9 cm
14-1/4"	36.2
29-3/4"	75.6

1 x 4   A

B   C

A

29-3/4"

1 x 4   B

3½"

14-1/4"

Build to overall dimensions noted

ASSEMBLED BASE

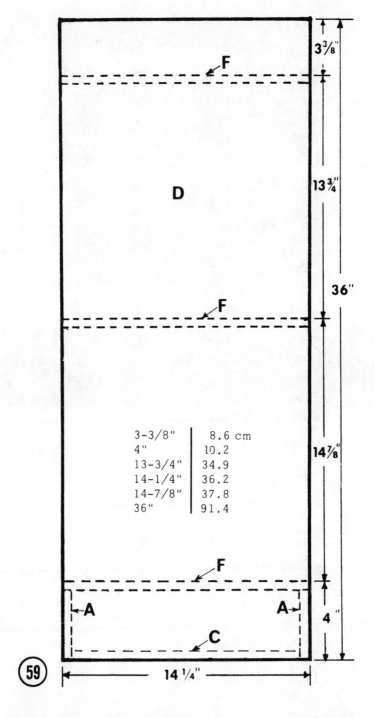

3⅜"

F

13¾"

D

36"

F

3-3/8"	8.6 cm
4"	10.2
13-3/4"	34.9
14-1/4"	36.2
14-7/8"	37.8
36"	91.4

14⅞"

F

A   A

C

4"

⑤⑨

14 ¼"

Cut two sides D, 14¼" x 36" from ½" plywood, Illus. 59.

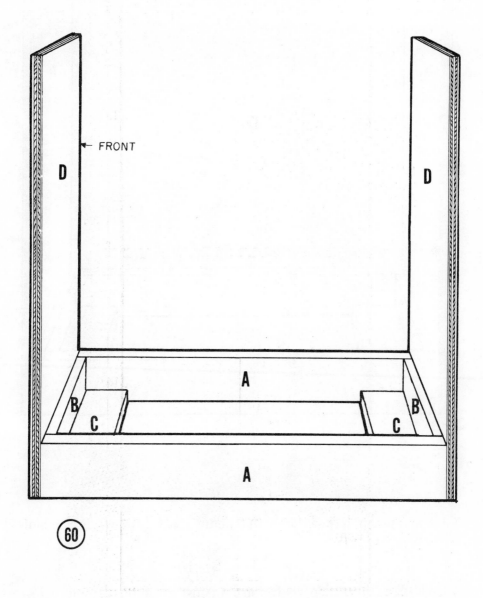

FRONT

D

D

A

B

C

C

B

A

60

Glue and nail D to base with 6 penny nails, Illus. 60.

Cut front E — ½" x 30¾" x 36".

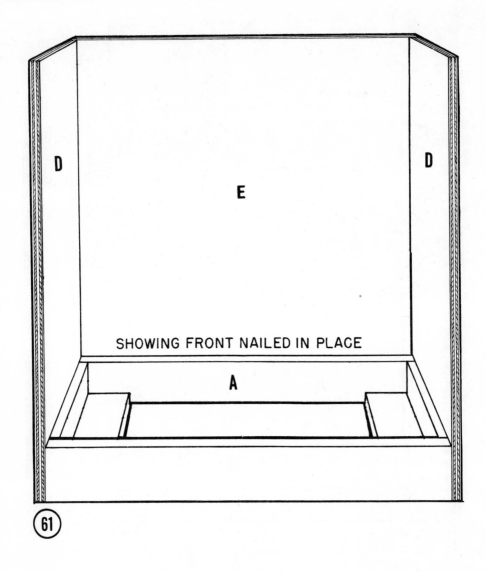

SHOWING FRONT NAILED IN PLACE

D   E   D

A

61

Glue and nail E in position with 6 penny nails, Illus. 61. Space nails 4″ to 6″ apart.

Check all additional parts for size against assembled frame before cutting.

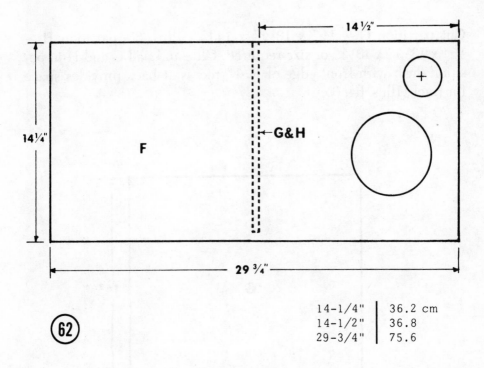

14 1/2"

14 1/4"

F

←G&H

29 3/4"

14-1/4"	36.2 cm
14-1/2"	36.8
29-3/4"	75.6

62

Cut three shelves F from ½″ plywood to size indicated, Illus. 62, or to size required. Cut ice and refuse holes in top shelf in approximate position indicated. Cut ice hole to size your ice bucket requires to set flush with F. Cut refuse hole to size a plastic container requires. Square or round plastic containers, available in most hardware stores, make good ice and refuse buckets.

Glue and nail D and E to shelves with 6 penny finishing nails in position indicated, Illus. 59.

Cut partition G — ½″ x 13¼″ x 14⅜″, Illus. 63; partition H — ½″ x 13¼″ x 13¼″, or size required. Glue and nail G and H in position flush with front edge of F. 1″ recess at back provides space for track, Illus. 64, 65.

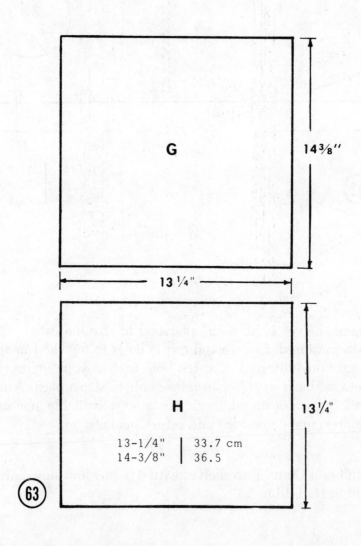

| G | 14⅜″ |

| 13 ¼″ |

| H | 13¼″ |

| 13-1/4″ | 33.7 cm |
| 14-3/8″ | 36.5 |

(63)

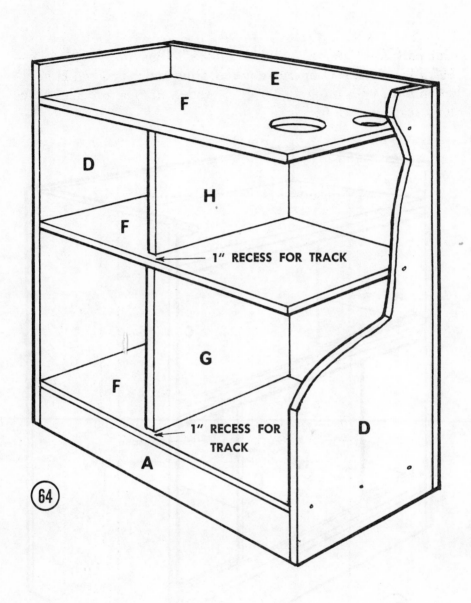

E

F

D

H

F

1" RECESS FOR TRACK

F

G

F

1" RECESS FOR
TRACK

D

A

64

53

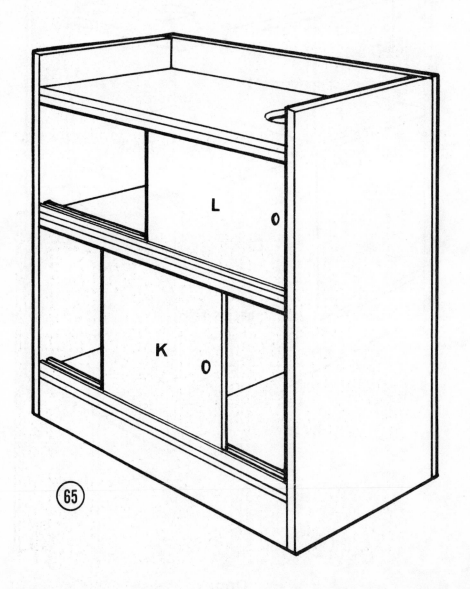

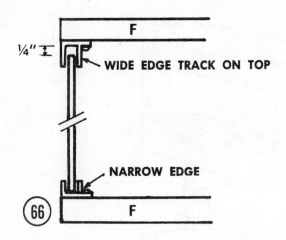

WIDE EDGE TRACK ON TOP

¼″

NARROW EDGE

F

F

66

Install ¼″ single sliding door track, Illus. 66, flush with back edge of F. Install wide track at top, narrow track at bottom.

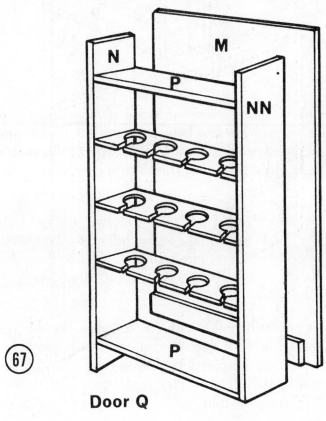

67

Door Q

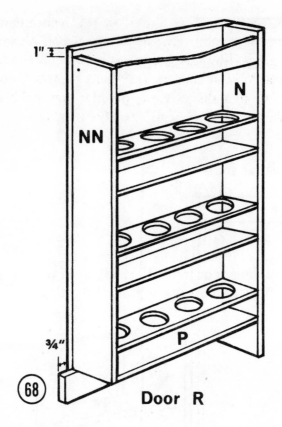

68 Door R

Cut ¼″ prefinished hardwood plywood for sliding doors K and L 15″ wide by height between track less ¼″, or amount track manufacturer specifies. Drill 1″ hole where indicated. Insert door in top track, drop into lower track. Trim door to fit.

Cut two M — ½″ x 15⅜″ x 36″; two N — ½″ x 4¼″ x 36″; two NN — ½″ x 4″¼ x 31⅜″; or size required. Cut shelves P from ½″ plywood to width required, Illus. 67, 68. Cut three shelves P to width of N-NN; one shelf for bottom of utensil box ¼″ less in width.

Temporarily nail N and NN to shelves P in position indicated. Glue and screw 1 x 4 x 15⅝″ cleat flush with bottom edge of M for door R. This cleat projects ¾″ beyond edge. Cut 1 x 4 x 13⅞″ for bottom of door Q. This cleat sets back from edge of M. Tack M in position to N-NN. Do not glue.

56

Doors Q and R can be fastened with 1¼″ or 1½″ continuous hinge. If you plan on finishing cabinet with ¼″ hardwood plywood, use 1½″ continuous hinge, Illus. 69. Temporarily fasten hinge to N and D with one screw at top and bottom. Test doors to make certain they fit. Trim if necessary, then dismantle, apply glue and nail N and NN to shelves. Apply glue and nail M to assembled N-NN.

Cut ⅜″ plywood to size required for glass racks. Cut holes and position glass racks to accommodate your glassware. Apply glue and nail N, NN and M to racks.

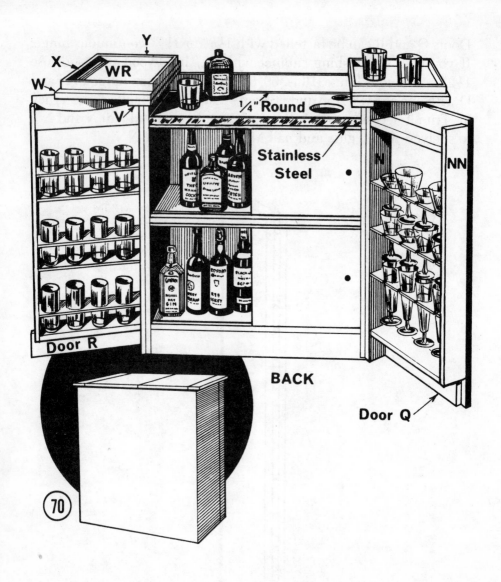

A utensil box, Illus. 68, can be built to size desired. Use ¼″ for face, ½″ plywood for bottom. Glue and nail in position 1″ down from top of M. Drive 4 penny finishing nails through M into bottom of box.

Cut two top cleats V, Illus. 70, ½″ x 3″ x 21⅜″. Place V in position. V projects ¾″ over E and D. Nail V temporarily in place. Fold two 21¼″ lengths of continuous hinge alongside V with butt edge up.

58

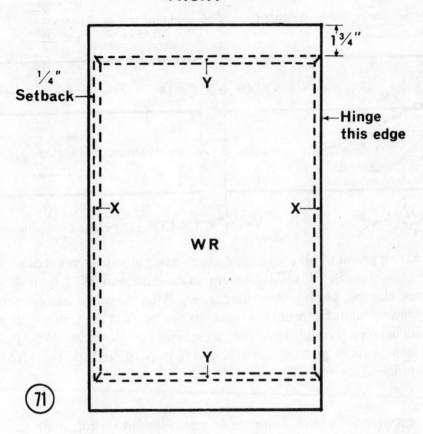

FRONT

1¾″

¼″
Setback

Y

←Hinge
this edge

X
X

W R

Y

⑦

Measure and cut top W — ½″ x 21⅜″ x 26½″, or length required. Cut W in half, Illus. 71, place alongside hinges. Trim if necessary.

Apply glue and nail V in position.   Countersink heads of nails and fill holes with matching Putty Stik.

Miter cut ends of four glass guards X and Y to overall size shown, Illus. 72, from ½″ x 1″ hardwood. Glass guards are optional. They could prevent glasses from slipping off bar if bar is moved when you are loaded. Bore holes through X and Y for 1¼″ No. 6 wood screws.

59

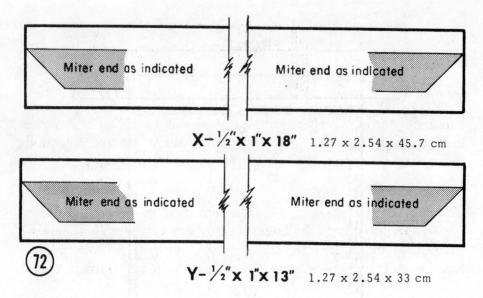

X—½" x 1" x 18" 1.27 x 2.54 x 45.7 cm

Y—½" x 1" x 13" 1.27 x 2.54 x 33 cm

Cut two pieces of plastic laminate to size required to cover area within glass guards, Illus. 73. Cement to underside of W. If you don't have clamps, use books or magazines. After laminate has set time adhesive manufacturer recommends, place X and Y in position, punch holes through laminate, so screws can penetrate W. Apply glue to ends of guards, screw X and Y in position with 1¼" No. 6 roundhead screws.

Cut a piece of plastic laminate to size required for top shelf. Carefully locate and cut holes for ice and refuse buckets. Apply adhesive and fasten laminate in position.

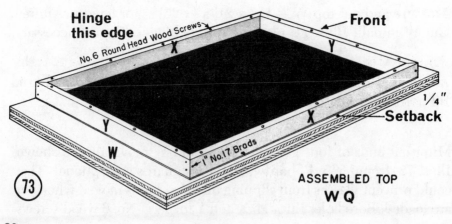

ASSEMBLED TOP
W Q

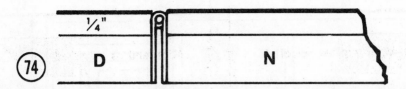

Cut 29¾", or length stainless steel or aluminum edging and fasten to shelf, Illus. 70. Cut ¼" stainless steel or aluminum quarter round to length required. Fasten in position around top shelf.

Fasten 1" or 1¼" hook to end of bottom shelf on door R and eye in position required to F. To keep cabinet doors closed with a "secret" catch, drill an ⅛" hole through center of both NN, 1" down from top. Cut a 6 penny common nail to 1¼". Insert nail through holes.

If you want to panel cabinet with ¼" prefinished hardwood plywood, cut panels to size required and apply with panel adhesive.

Cut two lengths of 1½" chrome or nickel continuous hinge 35½". Fasten hinge to N and D, ¼" up from bottom. Illus. 74 shows position of 1½" hinge when N is paneled with ¼" plywood.

After applying ¼" prefinished to W, fasten W to V.

All exposed edges can be finished with Wood Tape or equal paper thin veneer.

For that Mediterranean or Spanish effect, Illus. 57, miter-cut molding #111, Illus. 75, to length required, glue and brad in position to ½" plywood, or over ¼" prefinished.

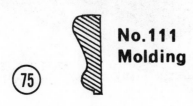

No.111 Molding

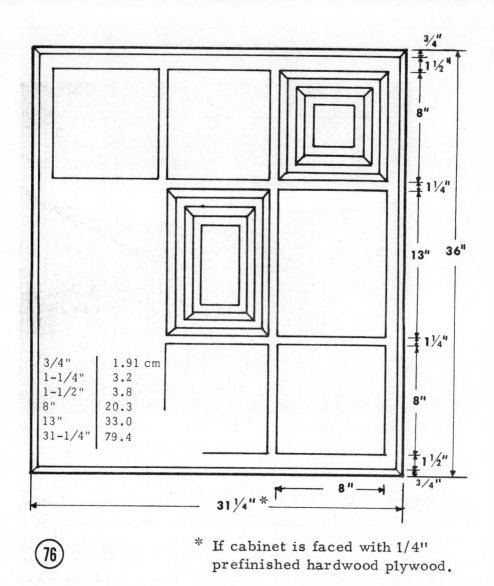

3/4"
1 1/2"
8"
1 1/4"
13"   36"
1 1/4"
8"
1 1/2"
3/4"

3/4"	1.91 cm
1-1/4"	3.2
1-1/2"	3.8
8"	20.3
13"	33.0
31-1/4"	79.4

8"

31 1/4" *

(76)   * If cabinet is faced with 1/4"
prefinished hardwood plywood.

Illus. 76 shows how molding first frames outside edge. If you apply #111 over ½" plywood, cut center panel to size required from ¼" plywood. This can be stained when molding and balance of cabinet is finished.

If you apply molding over ¼" prefinished, cut center panel to size required from ¼" prefinished plywood. Maintain ¾" spacings noted.

TABLE

(77)

Building this table, Illus. 77, could be the start of something big. It's ideal for guests regardless of what they drink. Since doctors, dentists, other professional and business people need plastic laminated tables in varying sizes, make one and you might be able to sell many others. Shipping costs from factory to retailer has risen to a point where you might be able to buy all materials to build this table for not more than it costs to pack and ship one.

1 — ¾" x 48" x 72" fir plywood
2 — 1 x 1 x 6′ square aluminum tubing
2 — ¼ x 1 No. 5 aluminum bar
2 — 5/4 x 3 x 8′ No. 1 pine
4 — ⁵⁄₁₆ x 3¼ carriage bolts — chrome or zinc chromate finish
8 — ⁵⁄₁₆ x 2¼ carriage bolts — chrome or zinc chromate finish
1 — 48" x 60" plastic laminate

Cut top A, 36 x 60, or size desired, from ¾″ fir plywood, Illus. 78.

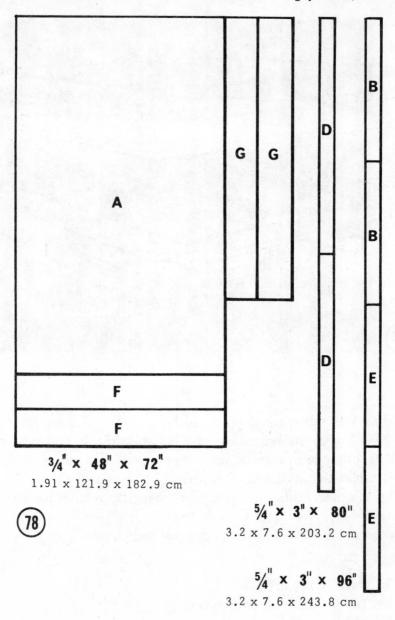

A

G G

D

D

B

B

E

E

F

F

¾″ x 48″ x 72″
1.91 x 121.9 x 182.9 cm

⑦⑧

5/4″ x 3″ x 80″
3.2 x 7.6 x 203.2 cm

5/4″ x 3″ x 96″
3.2 x 7.6 x 243.8 cm

Use 5/4 x 3 for cleats B, rails D, feet E, Illus. 79.

Use 1 x 1 square tubing for legs C.

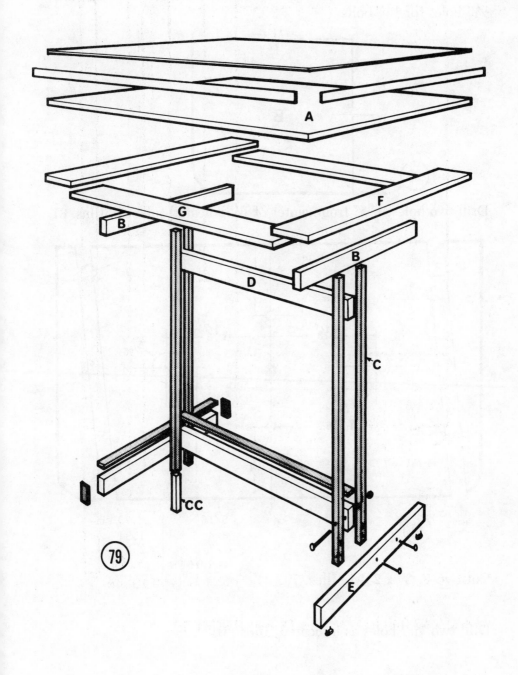

A

F

G

B

B

D

C

CC

79

E

65

Cut two B, 3 x 24, round bottom ends as shown full size, Illus. 80. Fasten with 5/16 or ¼" carriage bolts. Drill 5/16" holes for 5/16" bolts; ¼" holes for ¼" bolts.

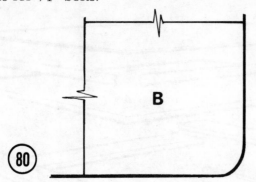

Drill two holes, 1⅛" from center of B, indicated full size, Illus. 81.

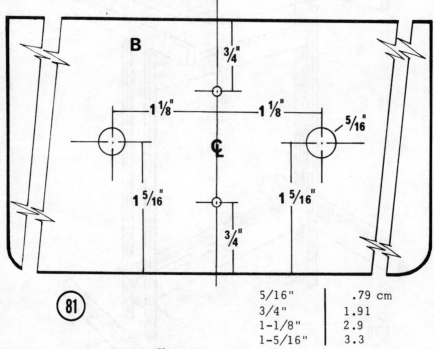

5/16"	.79 cm
3/4"	1.91
1-1/8"	2.9
1-5/16"	3.3

Cut two E, 3" x 23½", Illus. 79.

Drill two 5/16" holes as indicated, Illus. 81.

Cut two D, 3" x 39¾", Illus. 82. Drill holes where indicated.

66

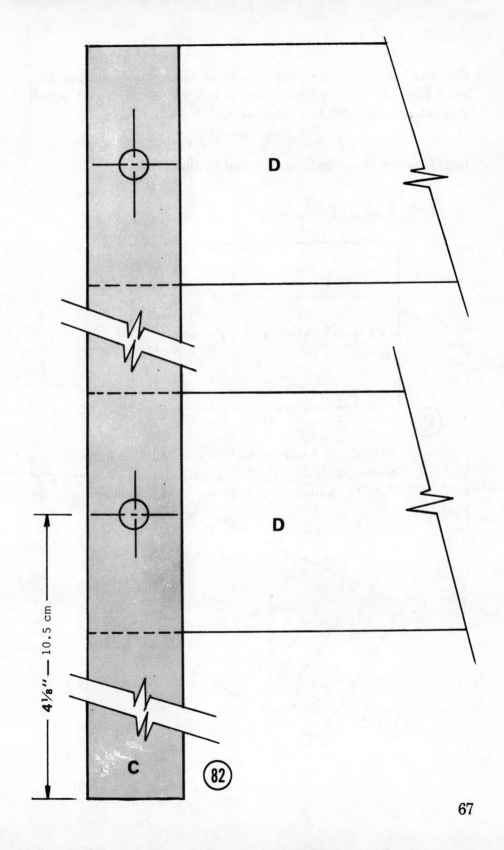

Cut four legs C, 1 x 1 x 29½" from square aluminum tubing. Cut eight filler blocks, ¾ x ⅞ x 6", insert in both ends of legs. Use full size pattern. Illus. 82, to locate and drill holes in C and D.

Legs C fasten to inside face of B and E, Illus. 79.

Drill holes through A, Illus. 83.

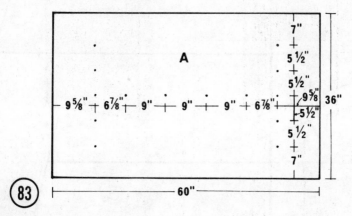

Apply glue to B, screw A to B with 1½" No. 8 flathead wood screws, Illus. 84. Countersink heads. Fill holes with wood filler. Apply glue and screw A to D. Nail B to D with two 8 penny finishing nails, Illus. 79.

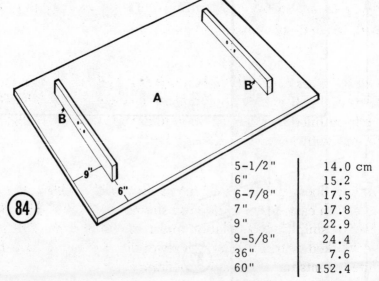

5-1/2"	14.0 cm
6"	15.2
6-7/8"	17.5
7"	17.8
9"	22.9
9-5/8"	24.4
36"	7.6
60"	152.4

Drill hole in C, size required to receive shoulder of bolt, Illus. 85. Bolt CDC with ⁵⁄₁₆ x 3¼″ aluminum or zinc chromate finished carraige bolts. Bolt E to C with ⁵⁄₁₆ x 2¼″ bolts.

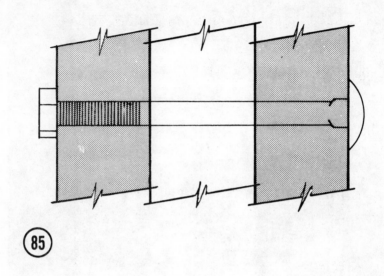

Cut four pieces of ¼ x 1 bar stock to fit end of E. Drill holes and nail or screw bar to feet. Cut two pieces, ¼ x 1 x 24″ bar. Drill holes and fasten bar to top of feet with No. 6, ½″ pan head aluminum screws. Cut a length of ¼″ bar 39½″. Drill holes and fasten to top of D, with four equally spaced 1″ metal screws.

Cut ¾″ plywood for F and G. Cut two F, 6″ x 36″; two G, 6″ x 48″. Glue and nail to top. Apply plastic laminate to top following directions outlined on page 83. Stain underside of A, B, D and E. Bolt B to legs with ⁵⁄₁₆ x 2¼″ carriage bolts.

Sliding doors can be fitted into almost any opening in a few minutes with easy-to-use aluminum sliding door track. The top track is deeper, simplifies installation and removal of door. This track may be worked with ordinary woodworking tools. All have handsome fluted fronts for a finished appearance.

BOOKCASE —RECORD CABINET BAR

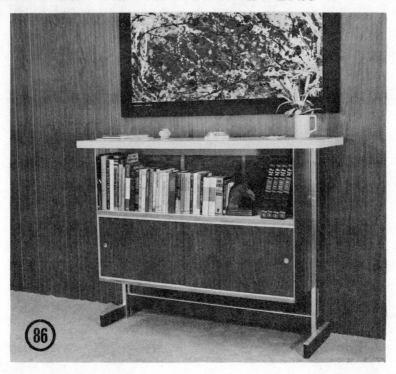

LIST OF MATERIALS

For Bar Measuring 18″ x 56½″

4 — 1 x 1 x 6′ aluminum square tubing
1 — ¾″ x 4′ x 6′ flakeboard
1 — ¼″ x 4′ x 8′ prefinished hardwood panel
2 — ¼″ x 1 x 6′ No. 5 aluminum bar
4′— Track for ¼″ panel doors
1 — ½″ x 6″ x 48″ fir plywood
4 — 1″ floor guides or 1″ domes of silence
1 — 36 x 60 plastic laminate

The bookcase bar, Illus. 86, was designed to serve many end uses. Books, records, a tape recorder or stereo record player can be installed on the open shelf while a sliding door cabinet provides ample storage for bottles and glasses. The plastic laminate counter makes an ideal snack bar. Read directions through completely. Note alternate method of construction.

Cut four 42″ legs, Illus. 87, from 1 x 1 aluminum square tubing.

Cut eight ¾ x ⅞ x 6″ filler blocks, Illus. 88. Insert filler blocks into legs so they finish flush with bottom and top edge.

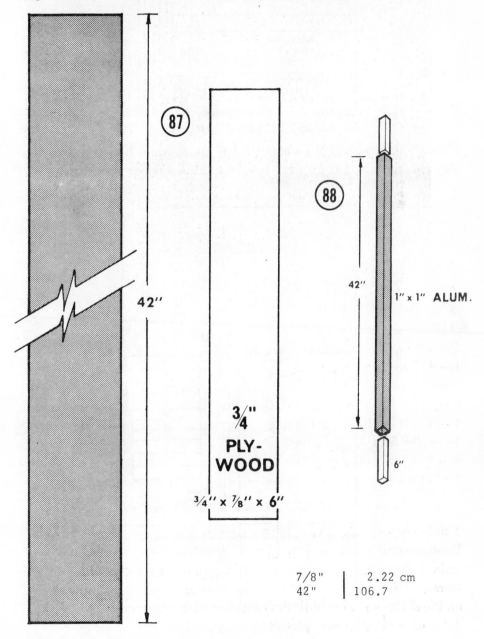

87

88

42″

42″

1″ x 1″ ALUM.

¾″
PLY-
WOOD

¾″ x ⅞″ x 6″

6″

7/8″	2.22 cm
42″	106.7

Illus. 89 shows a cutting chart for ¾″ flakeboard.

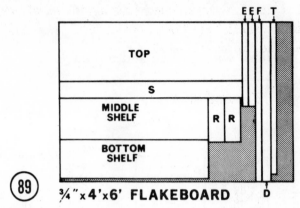

89 ¾″ x 4′ x 6′ FLAKEBOARD

Illus. 90 shows a cutting chart for ¼″ prefinished hardwood paneling. Cut parts when needed, to exact size your bar requires.

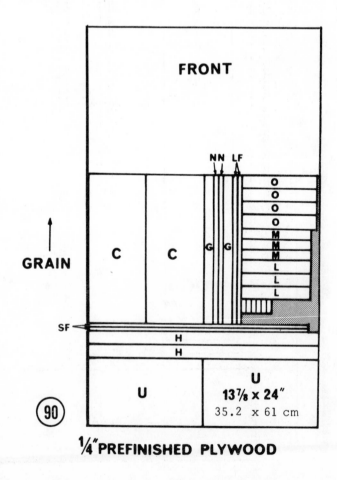

90 ¼″ PREFINISHED PLYWOOD

To simplify assembly, the two rear legs are designated A, the front legs B, Illus. 91. Place C with finished face against, and flush with edge of A. Drill holes 1½" up from bottom of C, and 1½" down from top. Space other holes 9" apart.

Fasten C to A with ¾" metal screws.

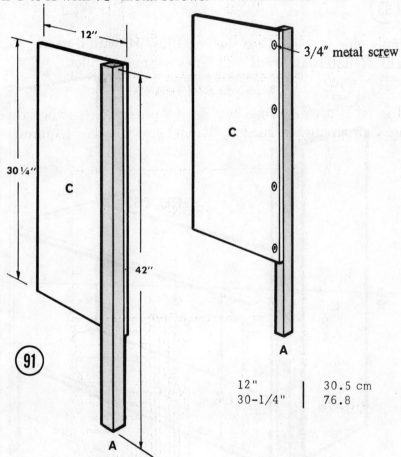

3/4" metal screw

12"	30.5 cm
30-1/4"	76.8

Cut bottom and middle shelf to size indicated, Illus. 92.

11-3/4"	29.8 cm
46"	116.8

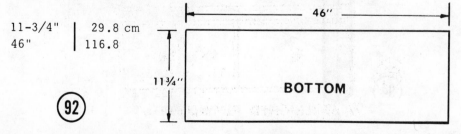

BOTTOM

Notch middle shelf where indicated, Illus. 93.

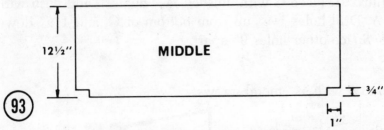

Apply glue and nail C to shelves, Illus. 94, with 6 penny finishing nails. Countersink heads. Fill holes with wood filler.

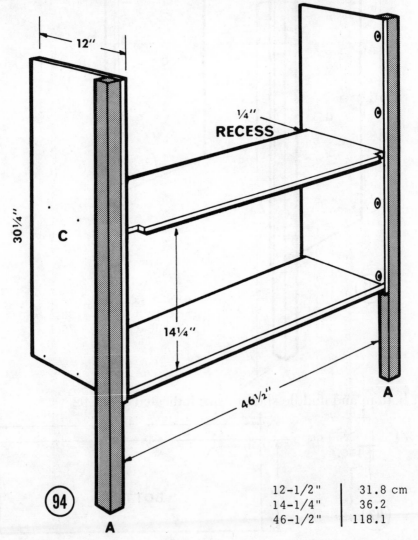

12-1/2"	31.8 cm
14-1/4"	36.2
46-1/2"	118.1

C projects ¼" beyond back edge of shelves. Finish back edge of shelves with a strip of ¼" x 1" prefinished paneling — SF, Illus. 90.

Cut D E F from ¾" flakeboard. Cut one D — 2¾ x 48"; cut two E, 2" x 25½"; one F, 2" x 48, Illus. 89.

To permit fastening D E F to legs A, drill ⅜" holes, ⅜" deep in position indicated, Illus. 95, and shown full size in Illus. 96, 97. This permits using 1" metal screws.

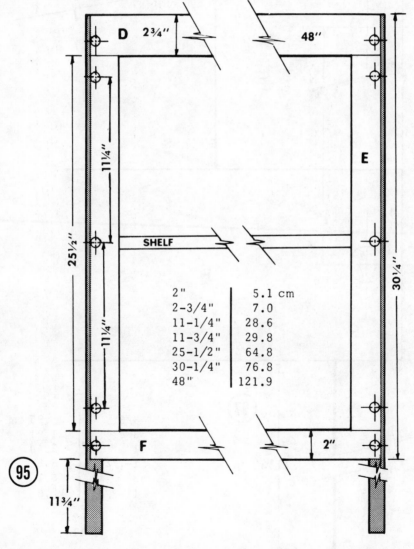

2"	5.1 cm
2-3/4"	7.0
11-1/4"	28.6
11-3/4"	29.8
25-1/2"	64.8
30-1/4"	76.8
48"	121.9

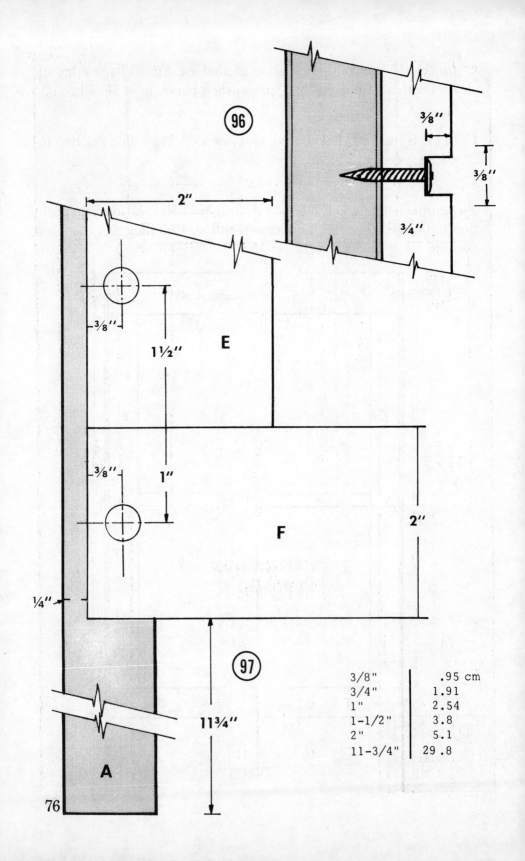

96

2"

3/8"

3/8"

3/4"

E

1½"

3/8"

1"

3/8"

F

2"

¼"

97

11¾"

A

76

3/8"	.95 cm
3/4"	1.91
1"	2.54
1-1/2"	3.8
2"	5.1
11-3/4"	29.8

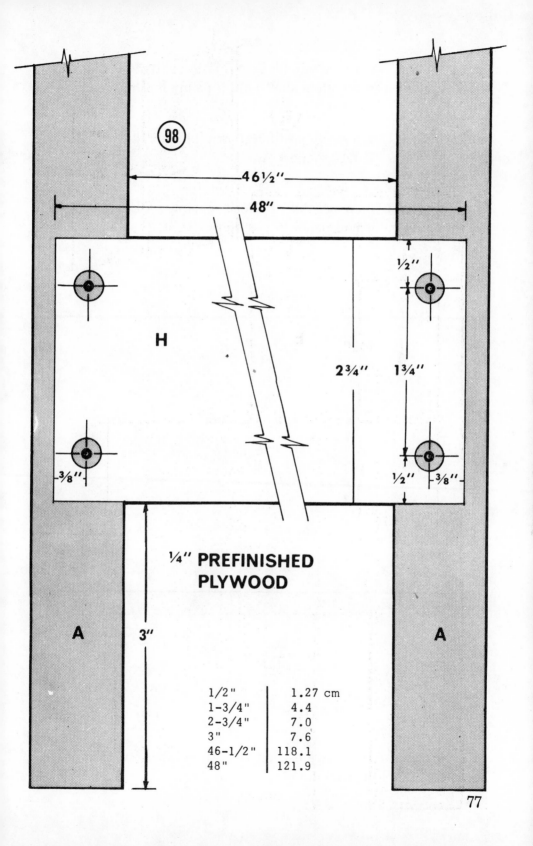

98

46½"

48"

½"

H

2¾"   1¾"

−3/8"

½"   −3/8"

¼" PREFINISHED
PLYWOOD

A   3"   A

1/2"	1.27 cm
1-3/4"	4.4
2-3/4"	7.0
3"	7.6
46-1/2"	118.1
48"	121.9

Drill through F, E and D into leg A and fasten parts ¼″ from edge. Nail through F into bottom shelf with 6 penny finishing nails.

Drill through H in leg A in position shown full size, Illus. 98. Fasten H to A with good face against A.

Cut ¼″ prefinished panel, 30¼ x 48 or size required, Illus. 99. Apply panel adhesive or nail panel in position to D, E, F and to middle shelf.

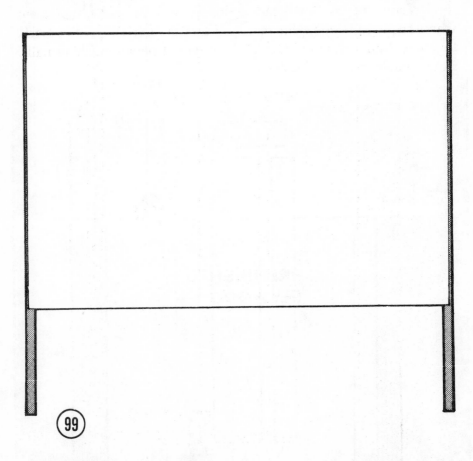

Keeping finished face against leg B, and recessed ¼″ from edge, screw G and H in position to legs B, Illus. 100.

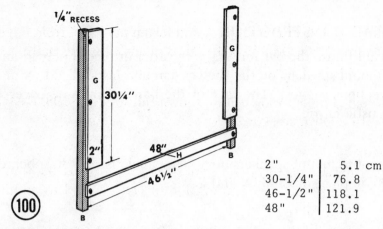

2"	5.1 cm
30-1/4"	76.8
46-1/2"	118.1
48"	121.9

Cut filler K, 2¾″ x 48″, Illus. 101, from ½″ plywood. To permit K to butt smoothly against head of screw, drill ⅝″ holes, ⅛″ deep where required. Apply glue to G and to both faces K. Clamp HKH together. Nail through G into D, E, F with 4 penny finishing nails. Countersink heads. Fill holes with wood filler.

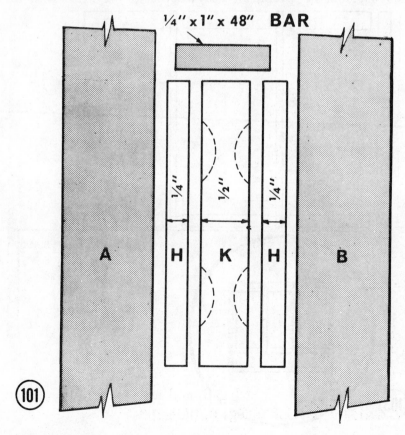

OPTIONAL CONSTRUCTION

If you want to use the bar for a tape recorder or record player, and wish to mount speakers on the shelves, cut and install L, M, N and L as directions suggest. The face of the bar can then be covered with acoustic fabric.

If you want to mount speakers on a face panel, use ¾″ flakeboard, Illus. 109, in place of L, M, N and L.

If you want to finish face of bar with a ¼″ prefinished panel, Illus. 110, you don't need L, M, N and L.

If needed, cut three L, 2¾ x 14″, Illus. 102, three M, 2 x 14″; two N, 1 x 30¼″, from ¼″ prefinished plywood.

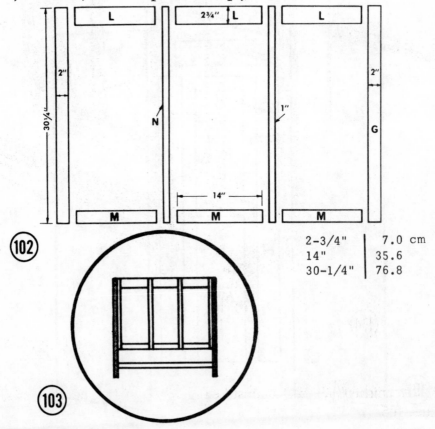

2-3/4"	7.0 cm
14"	35.6
30-1/4"	76.8

Nail in position to D and F with 1″ brads, Illus. 103. Stain exposed edges of L, M. N, or cover any exposed edges with matching wood tape.

Cut four O, 2¾′ x 15½″, Illus. 104, from ¼″ plywood; two filler P from ½″ plywood.

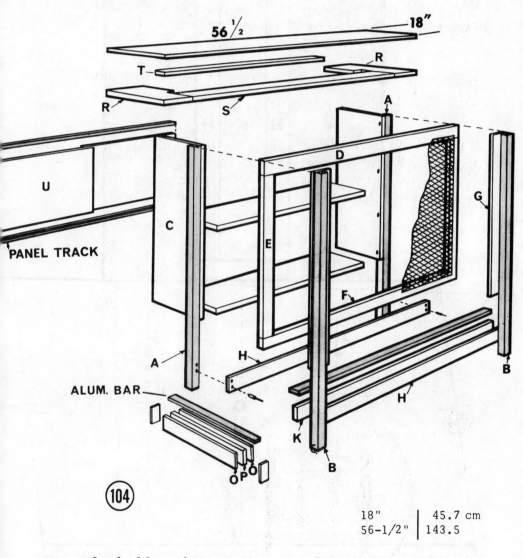

18"	45.7 cm
56-1/2"	143.5

Fasten finished face of O against Leg A and B with ¾″ metal screws, Illus. 105.

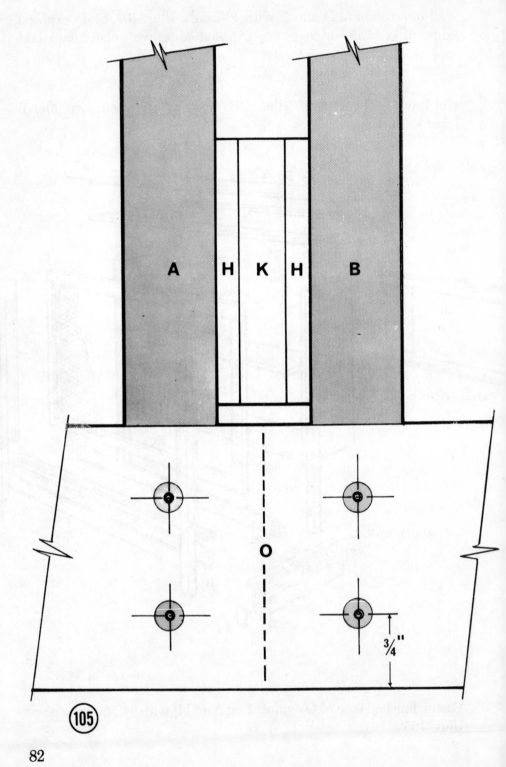

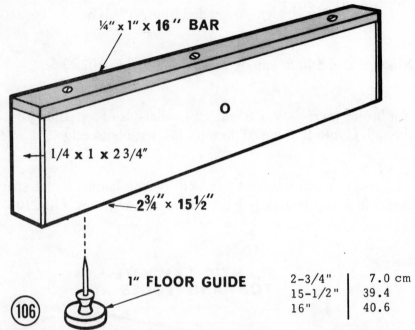

¼″ x 1″ x **16″ BAR**

1/4 x 1 x 2 3/4″

2¾″ x 15½″

1″ FLOOR GUIDE

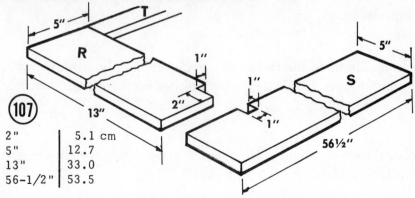

2-3/4″	7.0 cm
15-1/2″	39.4
16″	40.6

Chisel or drill a ⅝″, ⅛″ deep where required in P to receive head of screw. Apply glue to both faces of P. Brad and clamp OPO together. Cut and glue ¼″ pieces of plywood to ends of feet, Illus. 104, 106.

Cut top 18 x 56½″ from ¾″ flakeboard, Illus. 104. Apply glue, drill holes and screw top to D with 1½″ No. 8 flathead screws. Countersink screw heads and fill holes with wood filler.

Cut two R, one S, to size indicated, Illus. 107.

5″ T

R 1″

2″

13″

5″

1″ S

1″

56½″

2″	5.1 cm
5″	12.7
13″	33.0
56-1/2″	53.5

83

Cut one T — 1½″ by length needed from ¾″ plywood, Illus. 104.

Notch R and S to fit snugly around legs, Illus. 107.

Apply glue and screw R, S and T to underside of top, Illus. 104. Nail through C into R. Screw T to top flush with back edge.

To finish top and edges of bar with plastic laminate, cut strips of laminate A and B slightly larger than edge requires, Illus. 108.

PLASTIC LAMINATE
TOP AND EDGES

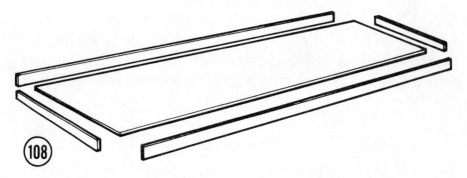

Apply adhesive according to plastic laminate manufacturer's directions. When adhesive sets, file or sandpaper edge of laminate flush with top.

Cut plastic laminate for top to size required. Apply adhesive and cement in position. Laminate on top finishes flush with laminate on edge.

Turn bar upside down on a flat, clean surface. Apply weight to permit laminate to bond securely to top.

Glue and brad 1″ strips of ¼″ prefinished hardwood paneling SF Illus. 108, to edges of shelf. When applying plastic laminate to shelves, laminate covers edge of ¼″ plywood facing.

Cut sliding door panel track to length required, Illus. 109. Install with wide track at top, narrow at bottom. Fasten in position with screws provided by manufacturer.

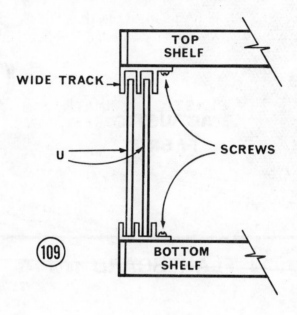

Cut door panels U, 13⅞ x 24″, Illus. 109. Drill ¾″ hole, 1½″ from edge of panel. Insert and fasten door pull following manufacturer's directions.

Cut ¼ x 1″ aluminum bar to length required, drill holes, screw bar to top of rail H with ½″ screws.

Cut ¼ x 1 aluminum bar to length required, drill holes, screw bar to top of feet, Illus. 106. Drive 1″ floor guides into center of K, 1½″ from outside edge.

If you wish to convert part of the bar into a cabinet for speakers, install ¾″ flakeboard panel in place of D, E, F. Cut panel to size required and fasten in position following procedure previously outlined. Saw openings for speaker units in position and to size required. Cover entire panel with acoustic fabric, Illus. 110.

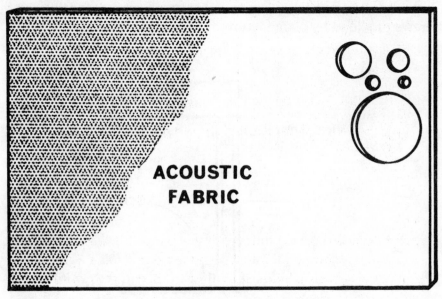

ACOUSTIC
FABRIC

¾″ FLAKEBOARD 30 ¼ x 48
76.8 x 121.9 cm

(110)

REVOLVING CABINET BAR

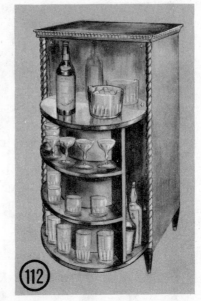

Originally designed as a Louis XIV sheet music storage cabinet, Illus. 111, we transformed it into a revolving bar. With a light touch the front panel reveals a hidden bar, Illus. 112, complete with "mixing shelf," glasses, and a semi-secret compartment for several fifths. Overall height 45″, 24″ width, 13″ depth.

LIST OF MATERIALS
1 — ¾″ x 4 x 8′ flakeboard — A, B, C, D, F, G, H, K, L, M
1 — ⅛″ nontempered hardboard — E, P, S, T
¼ lb. 3 penny finishing nails
¼ lb. 4 penny finishing nails
¼ lb. 6 penny finishing nails
Four 1¼ No. 7 flathead wood screws
16 x 25″ sheet aluminum
1 box of ¾ or 1″ aluminum nails
Two 4 ft. lengths #5 carved wood trim
Two 4 ft. lengths #111 or #30 French provincial trim
One pkg. four #111C or #30C corners
Four 4″ black legs
¼″ plate glass mirror — 21⅞ x 13¾″ (approximate)

87

Illus. 113 shows how to cut parts from ¾″ flakeboard.

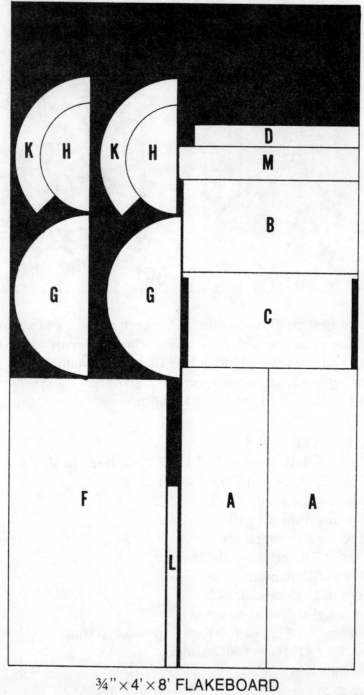

Cut two A, ¾ x 12 x 40¼"; one B and C, ¾ x 12½ x 24", Illus. 114. Notch C — ¾" deep to receive A in position indicated. Cut E — 24 x 41" from ⅛" hardboard.

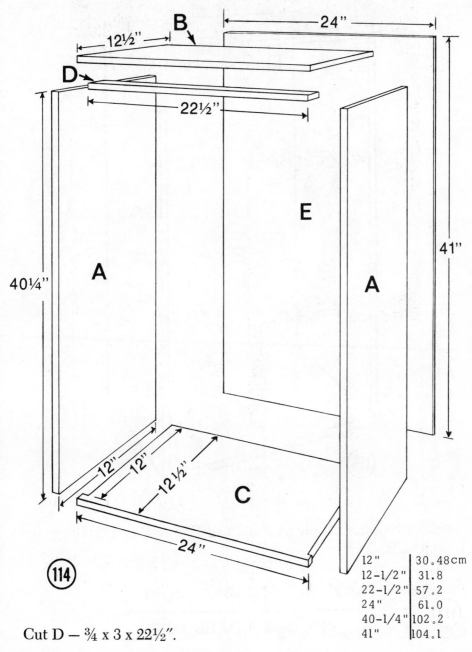

12"	30.48cm
12-1/2"	31.8
22-1/2"	57.2
24"	61.0
40-1/4"	102.2
41"	104.1

Cut D — ¾ x 3 x 22½".

Apply glue and nail A to C and B to A with 6 penny finishing nails every 3″. Countersink heads. Temporarily nail D flush with edge of B with 4 penny nails, Illus. 115.

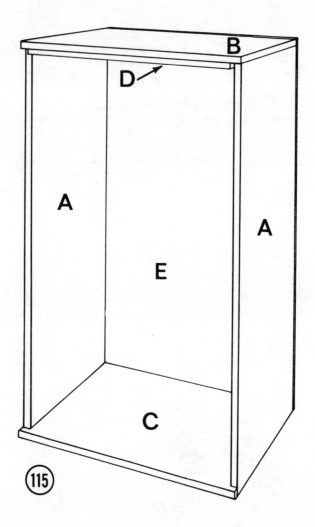

Check with square. Apply glue and nail E to A, B and C with ¾ or 1″ wire nails.

Cut revolving door F — ¾ x 21⅞ x 38½″, Illus. 119.

Locate and mark center of C, F and D, Illus. 116, 117.

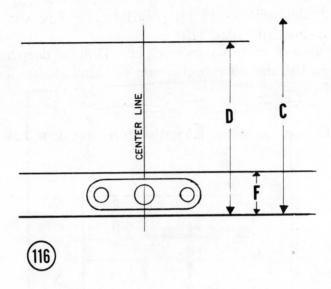

(116)

Install pivot door socket on bottom of door F and in D. Illus. 117, 118. Use screws provided by manufacturer.

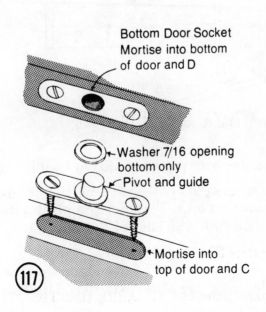

Bottom Door Socket Mortise into bottom of door and D

Washer 7/16 opening bottom only

Pivot and guide

Mortise into top of door and C

(117)

Center pivot on C and on top of F, Illus. 118.

Mark outline and mortise to receive plate. Drill ⅜″ deep hole to receive pivot. Use size bit manufacturer of hardware specifies, Illus. 116,117.

Remove D from cabinet and mortise to receive door socket, Illus. 117, 118.

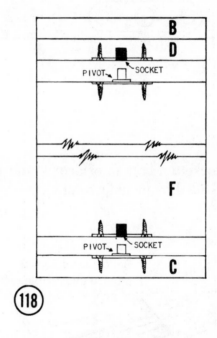

Screw pivot to C and to top of F, Illus. 118.

Place 7/16″ washer over pivot fastened to C, Illus. 117.

Turn cabinet upside down. Place door on pivot. Place D on pivot, slide D in position flush with edge of B, Illus. 119.

Screw D to B with four 1¼ No 7 flathead screws. Countersink screw heads. Apply leg mounting plates to C, Illus. 119. Turn cabinet right side up.

Apply leg mounting plates

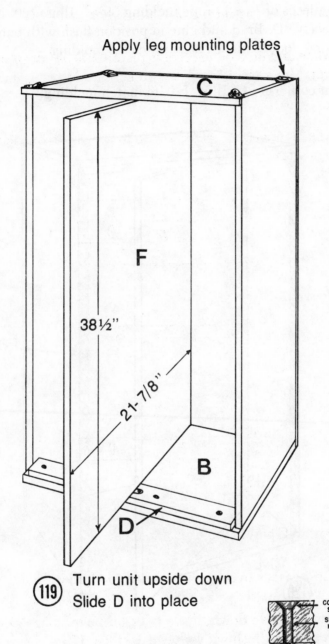

C

F

38½"

21-7/8"

B

D

(119) Turn unit upside down
Slide D into place

COUNTER SINK
SHANK HOLE
PILOT HOLE

| 21-7/8" | 55.6cm |
| 38-1/2" | 97.8 |

Cut two pieces of ½ x 1″ rope molding 39½″, Illus. 120. Notch top end to receive D. Brad and glue in position flush with outside edge of A. Swing door to make certain it clears molding.

File front corners of C, Illus. 120, to match molding.

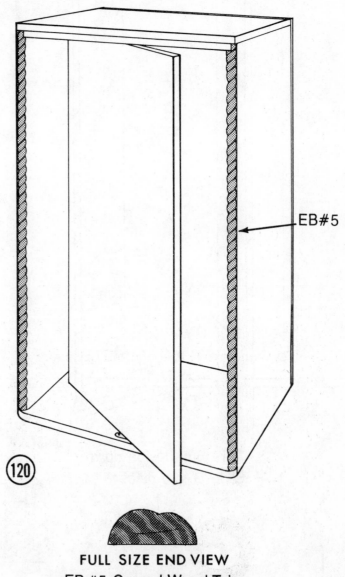

EB#5

FULL SIZE END VIEW
EB #5 Carved Wood Trim

When door operates freely, remove screws from socket in D and place door on bench.

Draw lines on inside face of F, Illus. 121, to outline location of shelves; and position of decorative molding on face.

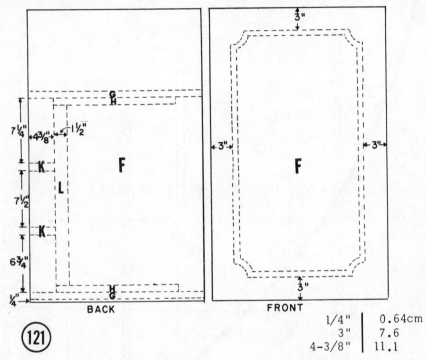

BACK   FRONT

1/4"	0.64cm
3"	7.6
4-3/8"	11.1

(121)

Cut two shelves G and two H to shape and size indicated, Illus. 122.

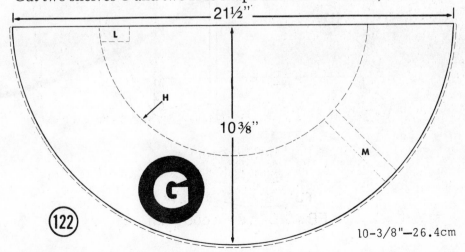

10-3/8"—26.4cm

(122)

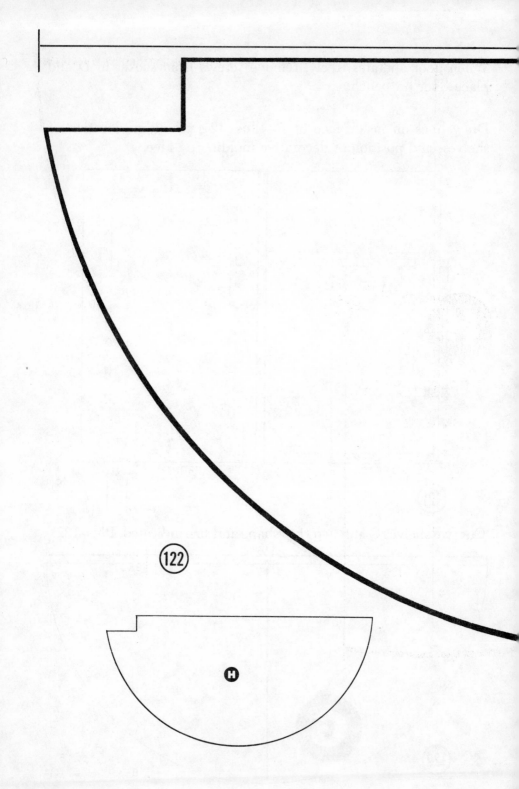

(122)

H

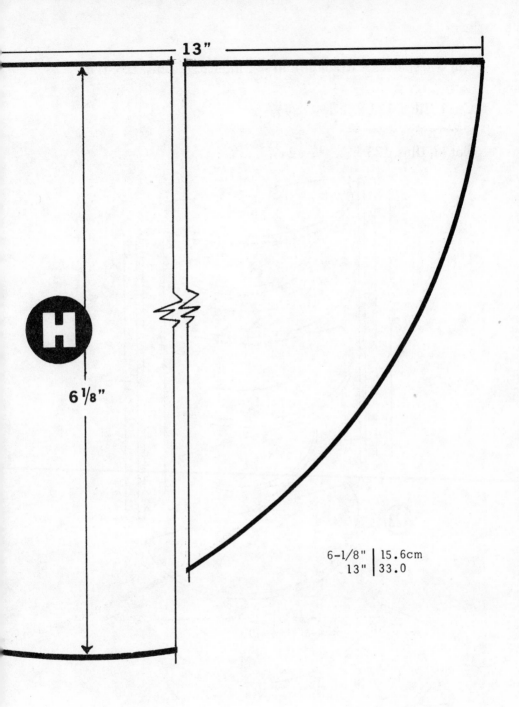

13"

6 ¹/₈"

H

6-1/8" | 15.6cm
13" | 33.0

Cut two shelves K to shape and size indicated, Illus. 123, 124.

Cut L, Illus. 123, ¾ x 1½ x 24½".

Cut M, Illus. 123, ¾ x 4¼ x 24½".

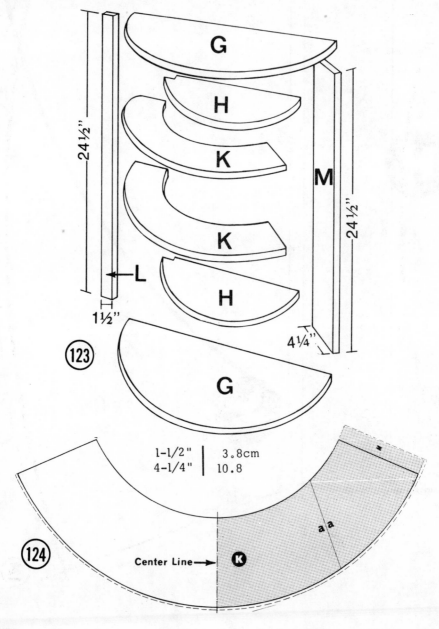

1-1/2"	3.8cm
4-1/4"	10.8

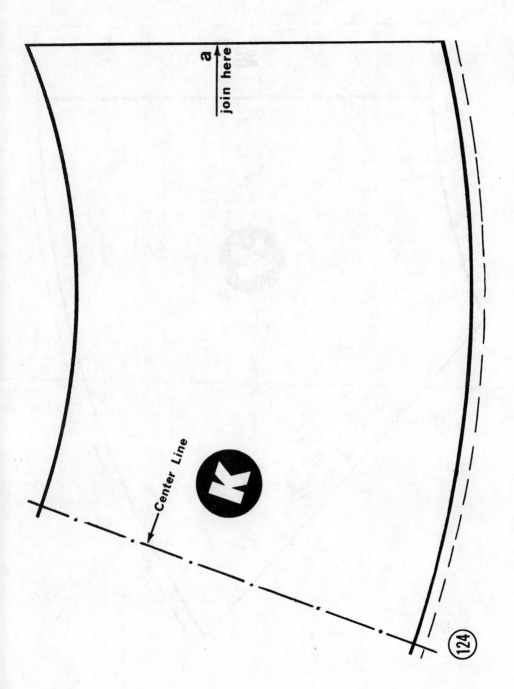

a
join here

Center Line

K

124

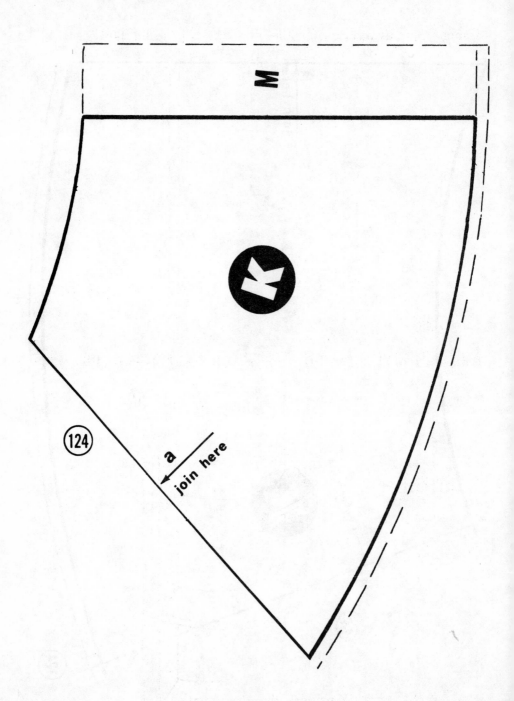

M

K

(124)

a
join here

Cut N, Illus. 125, 16 x 24½" from sheet aluminum.

Using a 3 penny nail, punch holes every 2", in position shown.

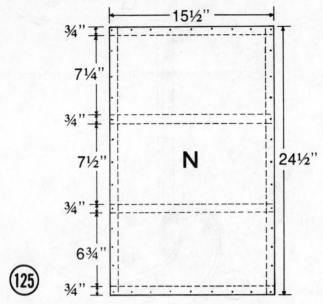

Glue and nail M to K with 6 penny nails, in position shown, Illus. 126.

3/4"	1.91cm
6-3/4"	17.1
7-1/4"	18.4
7-1/2"	19.1
15-1/2"	39.4
24-1/2"	62.2

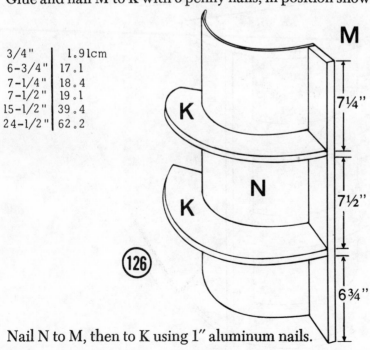

Nail N to M, then to K using 1" aluminum nails.

Glue and nail H to G in position shown, Illus. 122, 127. Use 3 penny finishing nails.

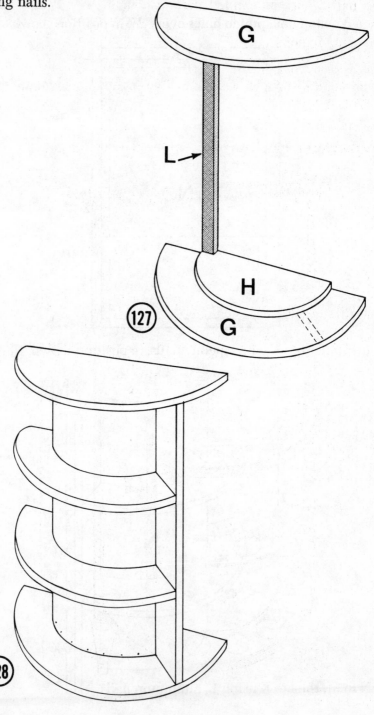

Glue and nail L to H with 4 penny finishing nails; G to L with 6 penny nails. Place assembled unit in position on G. Nail through holes in N into H. Nail N to L; G to M, Illus. 128. Cut aluminum off flush with edge of L.

Glue and nail F to G, H, K and L with 6 penny finishing nails, Illus. 129.

Apply provincial trim with precut mitered corners.

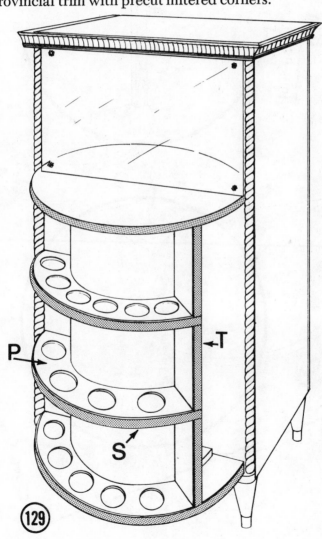

Miter cut and apply molding to top edge, Illus. 129. Cut 1″ wide strips of hardboard S, by length required. Nail flush with bottom edge of bottom G. Projecting edge provides lip on shelf. Nail strip flush with bottom of K; flush with top face of upper G. Cut ¾″ strip T, Illus. 129. Nail to edge of M. Use ¾ or 1″ wire nails.

Cut ⅛″ hardboard for glass holders, Illus. 129, 130. Cut holes to size and spacing required for base of your glasses. These are placed, do not nail, in position on G and K.

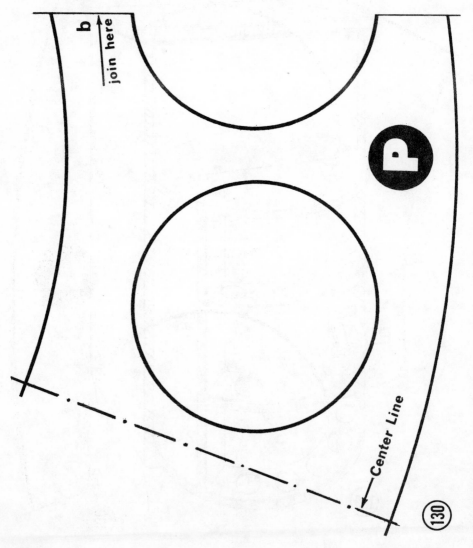

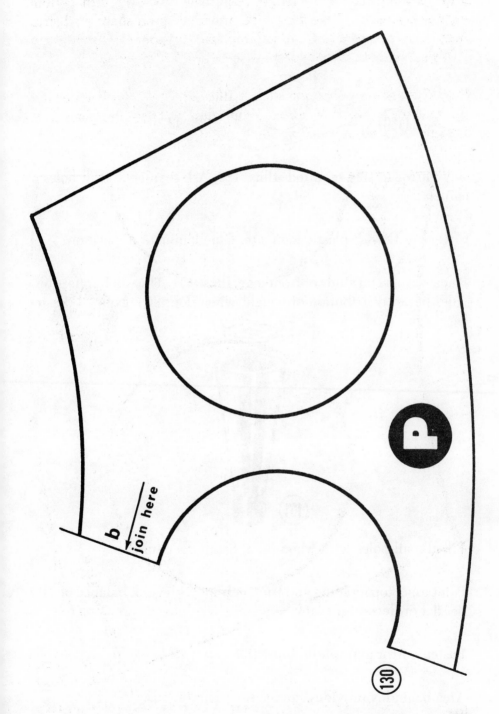

b

join here

P

(130)

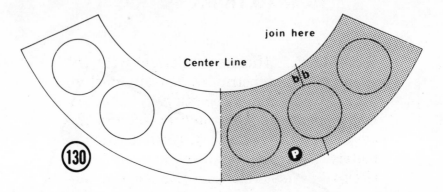

Buy mirror to size required, Illus. 129. Ask retailer to drill holes at corners.

Cover top G with plastic laminate. Glue laminate in position.

Place washers on studs of front legs, Illus. 131. This slight offset provides better distribution of weight when door swings open. Fasten legs in position.

Fill all nail holes with wood filler. Sandpaper smooth.

Paint rope, top molding and trim on front with gold, balance of cabinet flat or decorator black.

Fasten mirror in position, Illus. 129.

Area behind N provides storage for select brands.

HOW TO THINK METRIC

Government officials concerned with the adoption of the metric system are quick to warn anyone from attempting to make precise conversions. One quickly accepts this advice when they begin to convert yards to meters or vice versa. Place a metric ruler alongside a foot ruler and you get the message fast.

Since a meter equals 1.09361 yards, or 39⅜″ +, the decimals can drive you up a creek. The government men suggest accepting a rough, rather than an exact equivalent. They recommend considering a meter in the same way you presently use a yard. A kilometer as 0.6 of a mile. A kilogram or kilo as just over two pounds. A liter, a quart, with a small extra swig.

To more fully appreciate why a rough conversion is preferable, note the 6″ rule alongside the metric rule. A meter contains 100 centimeters. A centimeter contains 10 millimeters.

As an introduction to the metric system, we used a metric rule to measure standard U.S. building materials. Since a 1x2 measures anywheres from ¾ to ²⁵⁄₃₂ x 1½″, which is typical of U.S. lumber sizes, the metric equivalents shown are only approximate.

Consider 1″ equal to 2.54 centimeters;
10″ = 25.4 cm.
To multiply 4¼″ into centimeters: 4.25 × 2.54 = 10.795 or 10.8 cm.

INDEX TO MONEY-SAVING REPAIRS, IMPROVEMENTS, PATTERNS AND BOOKS
(Number designates EASI-BILD Pattern or Book)